*This book is about the spiritual power
that you can bring to your
bar/bat mitzv*

This book was rea

_____

YOUR NAME

*to prepare for my
bar/bat mitzvah ceremony.*

_____

Date

_____

Torah portion

_____

Name of synagogue and community

This book was a gift from

_____

Jewish Lights Books
by Rabbi Jeffrey K. Salkin

Being God's Partner:
How to Find the Hidden Link Between Spirituality and Your Work

A Dream of Zion:
American Jews Reflect on Why Israel Matters to Them

The Modern Men's Torah Commentary: New Insights from
Jewish Men on the 54 Weekly Torah Portions

Righteous Gentiles in the Hebrew Bible: Ancient Role Models for
Sacred Relationships

THE BAR/BAT MITZVAH SERIES

The Bar/Bat Mitzvah Memory Book:
An Album for Treasuring the Spiritual Celebration
(with Nina Salkin)

For Kids—Putting God on Your Guest List:
How to Claim the Spiritual Meaning of Your Bar or Bat Mitzvah

Putting God on the Guest List:
How to Reclaim the Spiritual Meaning of Your Child's
Bar or Bat Mitzvah

Bar/Bat Mitzvah Basics:
A Practical Family Guide to Coming of Age Together
(edited by Helen Leneman, foreword by Rabbi Jeffrey K. Salkin)

Bar and Bat Mitzvah's Meaning:
Preparing Spiritually with Your Child
(LifeLights Jewish pastoral care pamphlet series)

For Kids—

Putting God on Your Guest List, 2nd Edition

HOW TO CLAIM THE SPIRITUAL MEANING OF YOUR BAR OR BAT MITZVAH

Rabbi Jeffrey K. Salkin

JEWISH LIGHTS Publishing
Woodstock, Vermont

For Kids—Putting God on Your Guest List, 2nd Ed.:
How to Claim the Spiritual Meaning of Your Bar or Bat Mitzvah

2010 Second Edition, Quality Paperback, Second Printing

For information regarding permission to reprint material from this book, please mail or fax your request in writing to Jewish Lights Publishing, Permissions Department, at the address / fax number listed at the bottom of this page, or e-mail your request to permissions@jewishlights.com.

"In the Synagogue" by Cynthia Ozick is reprinted by permission of the author and her agents, Raines & Raines, 71 Park Avenue, New York, NY 10016.

Excerpts from *The Loman Family Picnic* by Donald Margulies reprinted with permission of Theater Communication Group.

© 2007 & 1998 by Jeffrey K. Salkin

The Library of Congress has cataloged the first edition as follows:

Salkin, Jeffrey K., 1954–
For kids—putting God on your guest list : how to claim the spiritual meaning of your bar/bat mitzvah / by Jeffrey K. Salkin.
     p.   cm.
Summary: A guide to preparing for the bar mitzvah or bat mitzvah, discussing the history and significance of this rite of passage and putting it in perspective with the core spiritual values of Judaism.
ISBN-13: 978-1-58023-015-5 (quality pbk.)
ISBN-10: 1-58023-015-6 (quality pbk.)
1. Bar mitzvah—Juvenile literature. 2. Bat mitzvah—Juvenile literature.
3. Judaism—Juvenile literature. [1. Bar mitzvah. 2. Bat mitzvah. 3. Judaism.]
I. Title
BM707.2.S24 1998
296.4'424—dc21   98-35465

Second Edition
ISBN-13: 978-1-58023-308-8 (quality pbk.)
ISBN-10: 1-58023-308-2 (quality pbk.)

10 9 8 7 6 5 4 3 2

Manufactured in the United States of America
Cover Art: Robert Lipnick

Published by Jewish Lights Publishing
A Division of LongHill Partners, Inc.
Sunset Farm Offices, Route 4, P.O. Box 237
Woodstock, VT 05091
Tel: (802) 457-4000   Fax: (802) 457-4004
www.jewishlights.com

Contents

PREFACE TO THE SECOND EDITION

It was back in 1992, and it all started with a scream.

"I can't take it anymore!" I exclaimed one Shabbat afternoon on the way home from synagogue. "Why is it that, week in and week out, I officiate at bar and bat mitzvah ceremonies and no one seems to 'get it'? Why is it that most of the adults and some of the kids themselves seem like they're on automatic pilot? There has to be another reason why people spend all this money and time and energy on bar and bat mitzvah, a reason besides 'It's a Jewish tradition.' How did they figure out that *this* Jewish tradition, of all traditions, should survive? Why do people care more about the party than the service? *What's going on here?*"

As you can imagine, I was pretty mad. I felt like a kid who was trying to play a game with a bunch of friends who didn't know or even care about the rules. Jews don't believe in simply being frustrated. No, when a Jew gets frustrated about something, there is a real possibility that the frustration will become a book. After all, that's what Theodor Herzl, the founder of Zionism, did when he sensed that the Jews of Europe were in trouble. He wrote a book calling for a solution. I'm not comparing myself to Herzl, but you get the idea.

And so, back in 1992, I wrote a book for Jewish parents called *Putting God on the Guest List: How to Reclaim the Spiritual Meaning of Your Child's Bar or Bat Mitzvah* (Jewish Lights Publishing), now in its third edition. That book taught Jewish parents how to "get with the program"—how to understand the real meaning of bar and bat mitzvah; how to appreciate the service; how to understand the meaning of Torah; how to find *mitzvah* projects for their families; how to celebrate with sense and sensitivity. And then I decided to write a kids' version of that book, which is the book you now hold in your hands.

Since then, these books have gone through a lot of printings, and I have had the joy of teaching about them in many communities in the United States and other countries. I'm happy that these books have helped thousands of families learn how to take bar and bat mitzvah seriously and how to make it all more meaningful. I'm also happy that wherever I taught this material, I met young people who had something to add to my teachings. Many of their insights are included in these pages.

I can predict how you might be feeling about your bar or bat mitzvah. You're probably feeling a little nervous about getting up in front of all those people. You may be dreading the hours of study that you're going to have to invest in preparation. There's also the slight possibility that you're a little bored or confused about the whole experience. Perhaps your teachers and parents haven't told you as much about your bar or bat mitzvah as you would have liked or found helpful.

Relax. You're not alone. Generations of Jewish kids have felt the same mixture of emotions that you are now experiencing.

The way I see it, you have a choice. You can choose to be confused and bored about the whole thing, or you can choose to figure it out and enjoy it. I sincerely hope that you make the second choice. You're going to remember your bar or bat mitzvah experience for the rest of your life, so you might as well make it the right kind of memory. Now you have a tool, in the form of this book, to help you spiritually connect with your bar and bat mitzvah.

I have one final note, a last word about an important word.

I use the word *spiritual* not only in the title of this book, but throughout its pages. Many Jews and non-Jews use the words *spiritual* and *spirituality* nowadays. What do they mean, anyway?

What do we say about someone who has a certain invisible "spark," and a good attitude toward life? "She's got a lot of spirit." When a bunch of athletes are working well together, they have a lot of "team spirit." When students feel strongly about their school, there's a lot of "school spirit." Summer camps have their own kind of "spirit."

When I use the word *spiritual* in this book, I mean the part of Judaism that's not just about doing rituals and learning, but about the *feeling* part of Judaism. It's like going to a sports event or a concert and really getting into it. It's like going to a parade and knowing why the parade is happening. Sometimes it's about the part of Judaism that gets us choked up or really happy. It's that moment when you say to yourself, "Now I understand why I'm doing all this stuff!" It's about "getting it."

This book will help you "get it."

Rabbi Jeffrey K. Salkin

ACKNOWLEDGMENTS

Sometimes it is very hard to know the precise moment when a book is born; sometimes it is very easy. I have no problem identifying when the idea for this book came into my mind.

In the autumn of 1997, I offered at my synagogue, The Community Synagogue in Port Washington, New York, a series of classes for parents on the spiritual meaning of bar and bat mitzvah. We discussed such issues as *mitzvah,* prayer, Torah, and the ethics of celebration. After we had been together for several weeks, a participant suggested that I try to teach our young people exactly what I had been teaching them.

The suggestion sounded a chord within me. Years before, I had written *Putting God on the Guest List: How to Reclaim the Spiritual Meaning of Your Child's Bar or Bat Mitzvah.* It is a book that teaches parents what they need to know in anticipation of their child's becoming bar or bat mitzvah. All along, I had been interested in refocusing parents into thinking more about God and Torah than about invitations and catering. The book, thank God, has been very successful in doing precisely that.

And yet, despite my years of working with bar and bat mitzvah candidates and their parents, I sensed that I had not yet fully addressed the issues of Jewish spirituality with them. I admitted that I had become as focused on peripheral bar and bat mitzvah matters as they had—except that my peripherals were such questions as "Can this boy read Hebrew well?" "Is this girl's *devar Torah* (a sermonette on the Torah portion) ready?" "Has this kid been coming to the required number of services that are necessary in order to become bar mitzvah in my synagogue?"

I needed to address the spiritual issues around bar and bat mitzvah for these young people—in ways that I had not yet done.

Therefore, this book, a modest offering in a very holy task: to make bar and bat mitzvah more real, deeper, and holier within our lives.

To Whom Am I Grateful?

I am grateful to my most recent congregation, The Temple, in Atlanta, Georgia. In my years as their rabbi, I committed myself to continuing to make the bar and bat mitzvah experience even deeper than it has been. They have been worthy partners in this sacred endeavor.

When I wrote the first edition of this book, several colleagues offered me suggestions: Rabbi Howard Buechler, a Conservative rabbi in Dix Hills, New York; Rabbi Elyse Frishman, a Reform rabbi in Franklin Lakes, New Jersey; Rabbi Richard Hirsh, a Reconstructionist rabbi in Philadelphia, Pennsylvania; Rabbi Neil Kurshan, a Conservative rabbi in Huntington, New York; and Rabbi Ned Soltz, a Reform rabbi in Arlington, Texas. Rabbi Frishman first told me about the *midrash* that Moses' sister Miriam was thirteen when she "stood up for Jewish survival" (which I quote in chapter 1). Rabbi Kurshan suggested the list of interview questions for parents and grandparents at the end of chapter 3. Rabbi Hirsh taught me some guidelines for *kashrut* (the Jewish dietary laws) in the Reconstructionist movement. For their friendship and collegiality, I am most grateful.

Arthur Magida was an extraordinary editor for the first edition of this book; over the years, his comments have helped me grow as a writer. None of this could have been possible without the enthusiastic support of my publisher, Stuart M. Matlins, founder of Jewish Lights Publishing. He has always been my partner in helping to raise the level of bar and bat mitzvah awareness, as he has raised the level of awareness in all things Jewish over the years. Emily Wichland, vice president of Editorial, has been particularly helpful in "staying on my case" and getting this second edition off the ground.

And finally, I am grateful to God. God, Who opens my eyes every day to the infinite possibilities of wisdom in the world. God, Who has brought me on this journey of faith and Who has made sure that my feet have not wearied. God, Who has implanted within me the hope that the words we leave behind are part of our immortality.

1

Beyond "Today I Am a Man/a Woman"

THE REAL HISTORY OF BAR AND BAT MITZVAH

*When I became bar mitzvah, my grandfather, Eleazar of
Amsterdam, of blessed memory, came to me one night in a
vision and gave me another soul in exchange for mine.
Ever since then, I have been a different person.*

—Shalom of Belz, Hasidic master

Let's get it right.

Bar or bat mitzvah is not an event or a ceremony, as in "When is your bat mitzvah?"

It is not a verb, as in "The rabbi bar mitzvahed me last year." It is not a past participle, as in "I was bat mitzvahed in that synagogue."

It is not something you have, as in "I am having my bar mitzvah next week."

Bar or bat mitzvah literally translates as "son or daughter of the commandment"—or, even better, as someone who is "old enough to be responsible for the *mitzvot*." A young person *becomes* bar/bat mitzvah simply by turning thirteen (or twelve for girls, in many Orthodox synagogues).

Becoming bar or bat mitzvah is a *rite of passage*. Every culture has rites of passage. In American culture, driver's education and passing the road test are rites of passage. Voting for the first time is a rite of passage. In fact, I felt something very powerful inside when I entered the voting booth for the first time. I felt like a mature participant in American democracy. In certain traditional African societies, a youth must kill a lion or wrestle with his father in order to prove his strength.

How can you tell what a culture values? Just look at the things that it celebrates through the rite of passage into adulthood. For Americans, driving and voting are important pieces of growing up; you can now get around and make your voice heard. For certain African cultures, physical strength is the most important thing.

But for us Jews, the most important thing is doing *mitzvot,* the obligations of Jewish life. *That* is what we celebrate as a rite of passage. Bar or bat mitzvah tells the community that you are no longer just a child but a mature Jew who is ready to take on religious responsibilities.

How Did Bar Mitzvah Begin?

Many famous Jews were never bar mitzvah, including Abraham, Isaac, Jacob, Moses, Aaron, and King David. There is a reason: The Bible doesn't care that much about adolescent rites of passage, except that Abraham's oldest son, Ishmael, was circumcised at the age of thirteen (Genesis 17:25).

On the other hand, there may be some "hidden" rite-of-passage ceremonies in the Bible. For instance, Genesis tells us that Abraham's wife, Sarah, could not have children, so she gave her handmaiden Hagar to Abraham so he could have children with her. The child that resulted from this union was named Ishmael. Sarah became increasingly disturbed by the continued presence in her household of Hagar and her son, and she persuaded Abraham to expel them into the wilderness, where a spring of water miraculously welled up in the desert and revived the almost dying Ishmael.

Maybe Ishmael's dangerous wilderness ordeal was an ancient Middle Eastern rite of passage, like an Outward Bound camping experience. The ritual could have meant this: A boy is growing up. He is tested in the wilderness to see whether he can survive. In this way, his childhood "dies" and his adulthood is "born."

There may even be a rite of passage in Genesis's famous story of the binding of Isaac, which we read in synagogue on Rosh Hashanah morning. God told Abraham to offer Isaac as a sacrifice on Mount Moriah, but an angel intervened to save the boy's life, and Abraham sacrificed a ram instead. This is what the ritual could have been: A father saw that his son was growing up. The father deliberately placed his son in danger; the boy almost died and then was miraculously saved so he could advance toward maturity.

This is a pretty brutal way to enter maturity. But think about it: The bar and bat mitzvah experience certainly *feels* like a trial, although it is much less dangerous than Ishmael's or Isaac's! Look at it this way: A young person is growing up. The child struggles with learning Torah and then has to present it to a community. It is a test, of sorts.

It feels wonderful to be tested—and to pass the test. A man who converted to Judaism told me that when he was a teenager in Wisconsin, the local rite of passage was being allowed to hunt with the men for the first time: "I remember what it was like to hold the rifle for the first time, and to be surrounded by older boys and grown men. It was a real test."

So Where Does Bar Mitzvah Come From?

To find the origins of bar mitzvah, let's go back in Jewish history to the rabbinic period.

Right after the Jewish people returned from exile in Babylonia in the fifth century B.C.E., Jewish sages began to interpret the Torah and find new meaning in its words. Over the centuries, their interpretations of the Torah (the *written* law) formed the basis of Judaism's *oral* law. Those interpretations of Torah—and the further interpretations over the centuries of *those* interpretations—created the Judaism that we know today.

The earliest code of Jewish law is the Mishnah, which was compiled about the year 200 C.E. One of the most important sections of the

Mishnah is called *Pirke Avot,* "the chapters of the fathers." *Pirke Avot* is a collection of sayings that illustrate how the ancient sages saw the world and how they interpreted the responsibilities of being a Jew.

The real "inventor" of bar mitzvah was the second-century C.E. sage Judah ben Tema. In *Pirke Avot,* Judah imagined a timeline of Jewish life:

> At five, one should study Scripture;
> at ten, one should study Mishnah;
> at thirteen, one is ready to do *mitzvot;*
> at fifteen, one is ready to study Talmud [the commentary on the Mishnah];
> at eighteen, one is ready to get married;
> at twenty, one is responsible for providing for a family.
>
> —Mishnah, *Avot* 5:24

What was the meaning of Judah ben Tema's timeline? At every step of life's path, we have responsibilities to fulfill. That is how Judaism imagines life: an unfolding series of obligations to the community and to ourselves.

But the real origins of bar mitzvah come from *midrash,* the name of the kind of story that the ancient rabbis told about characters in the Bible. Telling *midrashim* was how the rabbis continually breathed new life into Torah and found new meanings in its stories.

What do the *midrashim* say about the significance of the age of thirteen?

Consider one of the most famous Jewish stories in all our sacred literature. Abraham's father, Terach, is in the idol business in Ur, a city in ancient Sumer. (I like to joke that he owned a chain of idol stores called "Gods R Us.") He goes away on business and leaves his young son Abram in charge of the idol shop. Abram, who is later called Abraham, shatters all the idols in the store with a stick, then places the stick in the hand of the largest idol. When Terach gets back, he sees the ruined merchandise.

"What happened?" he demands.

"Oh, father, it was terrible," says Abram. "The small idols got hungry and started fighting for food. Then, the large idol got angry and broke the smaller ones into little pieces. It was frightening. I don't want to talk about it."

"Wait a second," says Terach. "Idols don't get hungry. They don't get angry. They don't speak. They're just . . . they're just clay idols."

"So," Abram asks with a smile, "why do you worship them?"

Why does Abram do this? Because he wants to make a bold statement that idols are worthless. Just as Alexander Graham Bell invented the telephone, and Edison invented the light bulb, Abram "invents" monotheism: the idea that there is only one true God.

Abram was thirteen when he smashed those idols. Thirteen, in fact, is a very good age for idol-smashing. It's when young people begin to develop independent thinking. Idols are more than gods of wood and stone. An idol is anything that is *not* God that we worship *as if it were* God. These might be material things, like cars or stereos, or they might be popularity or perfect test scores. You can start smashing your own idols when you reach thirteen.

In one of the most religious conversations I ever had with a teenager, a thirteen-year-old told me she did not want to celebrate becoming bat mitzvah in the synagogue. I was not happy about her decision. But, as we spoke it was apparent that this was something she had seriously and deeply considered.

"Rabbi," she said, "I like learning Hebrew, so I'm not nervous about that. I like religious school, and I will go on to confirmation. I just don't want to become bat mitzvah."

What did she tell me? She said that she didn't like what bat mitzvah had become for so many of her peers. The parties, the social pressures, the competition, and the fanciness turned her off. I reminded her that she did not have to imitate what her friends and peers did.

She still refused to go ahead with the ceremony. In doing so, she clearly wanted to make a statement.

I reminded her that bat mitzvah was what she would *become,* simply by becoming thirteen. Moreover, I assured her that her decision was not a done deal. While thirteen is the traditional age of bar and bat mitzvah, many Jews celebrate that rite of passage when they are older—sometimes later in their teens, or in college, or as adult *b'nai* or *b'not mitzvah.* There are adults who were never bar or bat mitzvah when they were thirteen, either because they are women and did not have the opportunity; or Jews-by-choice, also known as converts, who were not Jewish at thirteen; or simply because they didn't want to at that stage in life. So, they can "become" bar and bat mitzvah publicly later in life, even though you automatically become bar or bat mitzvah at the age of thirteen.

I also said that I was proud of her. Reminding her of the legend about Abraham shattering his father's idols, I told her that according to tradition, Abraham had done this when he was thirteen years old. "Maybe you are shattering the idol that bat mitzvah has become for so many of your peers. Maybe today you really *were* bat mitzvah after all—in the true, ancient meaning of the term."

She smiled. Sure enough, she did not have a bat mitzvah ceremony. But she stayed in religious school, and she was confirmed with the other members of her tenth-grade class. At her confirmation, I reminded her that she was a true daughter of Abraham, the first of the great idol smashers. That moment of idol smashing was the only bat mitzvah ceremony that she ever needed in order to become a mature Jew.

Another *midrash* says that, at the age of thirteen, Jacob and Esau, who were twins, went their separate ways: Jacob to the worship of God, Esau to idolatry. Each followed his true nature and inclinations. God wants us to do the right thing. But God cannot make us do the right thing. Only *we* can make ourselves do the right thing. And bar and bat mitzvah is the age to start doing just that.

According to a *midrash,* Miriam was thirteen years old when she arranged for her infant brother Moses to be adopted by Pharaoh's daughter, thus ensuring his survival and the survival of the Jewish people.

Finally, the Talmud says that Bezalel was thirteen when he designed the ancient tabernacle for worship in the wilderness.

Thirteen: The Age of Choices

You already know that you have to recite certain prayers and read certain texts at the ceremony when you become bar or bat mitzvah. But in traditional Judaism, fathers have their own prayer to say. This is what it is: *Baruch she-petarani me-onsho shel zeh*—"Blessed is the One Who has now freed me from responsibility for this one."

What does that prayer mean? It means that the father is no longer responsible for his son's sins.

But there is something deeper than that. Most prayers begin *Baruch attah Adonai, eloheynu melech ha-olam.* The prayer above omits *Adonai, eloheynu melech ha-olam.* It omits any mention of God!

This is not a happy prayer. It is a *sigh.* It reminds us that there are limits to what even good, committed parents can do with their children. The rest is up to the child himself or herself. When parents say *Baruch she-petarani,* they say, in effect, "Whatever this young person does now, he is legally and morally responsible. Thank God, it's not my responsibility."

At that moment, every Jewish parent can become Isaac, who, upon looking at his sons Jacob and Esau, realized that he had done all that he could for them. One son would worship God; the other would worship idols. There are limits to every parent's hopes and dreams, limits to every parent's ability to control and influence. The rest is up to faith, hope, and trust.

But there is another opinion about the meaning of *Baruch she-petarani.* Maybe the parent doesn't say this about the child. Maybe the *child* says this about the *parent!* Maybe the prayer is said by the child at this transitional moment as a way of stating, "I am my own person, and my parents are their own people. We are no longer attached to each other. We are each responsible for ourselves."

Thirteen is the traditional age of spiritual and moral choices. At thirteen, you become endowed with both the *yetser hatov* (the "good inclination") and the *yetser hara* (the "evil inclination"). These dueling forces are in each of us. Now you can begin to ascend to the good and the holy.

Thirteen is also the traditional age of religious achievement. A thirteen-year-old can help constitute a *minyan* (the quorum of ten adults traditionally needed for communal prayer). Traditionally, only men were counted in a *minyan,* and this is still the case in Orthodox and some Conservative communities. Reform, Reconstructionist, and the overwhelming majority of Conservative synagogues count women as part of the *minyan.*

In addition, a thirteen-year-old can also fast on Yom Kippur. A minor tractate of the Talmud, *Sofrim,* mentions that in the era of the Second Temple (approximately the first century of the Common Era) there was a ceremony for twelve- or thirteen-year-olds who had completed their first Yom Kippur fast. In the ceremony, the elders of the community blessed the children on the occasion of completing this important *mitzvah.* Perhaps *this* was the first real Jewish coming-of-age ceremony.

Historically, thirteen also became the age of a kind of legal maturity. The Mishnah says that the vows of a boy age thirteen plus one day are legally binding. At thirteen, a youth could be a member of a *bet din* (a Jewish court) and could buy and sell certain items of value.

There is yet another opinion about the origin of bar mitzvah. When a Jewish boy is eight days old, his family celebrates the *brit milah* (ritual circumcision) ceremony. At that ceremony, the father says, "As we have brought this child into the covenant of Abraham, so, too, will he be brought into the study of Torah, the *chupah* [the wedding canopy], and the performance of good deeds." Here's a new idea about the meaning of bar mitzvah. At the bar mitzvah ceremony, presumably those people who were at the *brit* ceremony are back again. Quite possibly, the last time they were all together was at the *brit* ceremony. They heard the father promise then that his son would eventually study Torah. And now, thirteen years later, look! That prayer has become a reality! "Here we are, thirteen years later. Our dream has come true. This former little kid now knows a little bit of Torah."

Bar mitzvah, therefore, is a passage not only for the child. It is also a passage for the father (and in modern times, for both parents). It means that they have fulfilled their Jewish responsibility to the child and to the Jewish community.

How Did Bar Mitzvah Customs Evolve?

Don't think that children were not allowed to perform *mitzvot.* Of course they were. But a child who was younger than thirteen years old performed *mitzvot* only as *options.* Once he turned thirteen, he performed them as *obligations.* As the Talmud taught, "It is better to do something when you're commanded to do so than to do something when you're *not* commanded to do so." The supreme value in Jewish life is *being commanded.* Doing things just because you feel like doing them is really no big deal. You could just as easily decide *not* to do them. Because the state of being commanded is a sacred state, it deserves celebration.

Jews sensed this, and during the early Middle Ages (1000 C.E.–1400 C.E.) their practices began to change. They began to realize that religious life demands maturity. Judaism is not just kid stuff.

Within a short time, young children could no longer wear *tefilin* (the leather boxes worn on head and arm that contain sacred verses from the Torah, also known as phylacteries) or be called for *aliyot* to the reading of the Torah. These honors were reserved for Jewish adult males and later became the essential features of the bar mitzvah observance. In the sixteenth century, it became customary to call a boy to read the Torah on the Shabbat that coincided with his thirteenth birthday or that closely followed that birthday. He read the last section of the Torah portion for that Shabbat, called the *maftir.* He also read the weekly section from the Prophets section of the Hebrew Bible, called the *haftarah.*

When did bar mitzvah really become important to Jews? In medieval Spain. The Jews of medieval Spain had a brilliant culture. For them, it was a true Golden Age. Jews like Shmuel Ha-Nagid and Isaac Abravanel rose to political power. Moses ibn Ezra and Yehuda ha Levi wrote beautiful poetry. Moses Maimonides wrote the greatest Jewish philosophical work of all time. Moses de Leon wrote the Zohar, the holiest book of Jewish mysticism. The Golden Age of Spain produced philosophy, mysticism, art, literature, astronomy, astrology, music, and ethical reflection.

Suddenly, that beautiful culture came to an end. The Christians began to reconquer Spain from the Muslims. In 1391, there were anti-Jewish riots. In the wake of those acts of violence, one-third of the Jews of Spain converted to Christianity. They were called *conversos,* or New Christians. They were also called Marranos. Many were sincere Christians. But many others secretly practiced the faith of their ancestors. They met in cellars, where they secretly lit candles, ate *matzah,* and taught their children about Judaism.

Bar mitzvah became a crucial time for Marrano families: it was the moment when they told their children that they were Jewish. If the children had been informed of this earlier, they might not have been able to keep the secret. They would have endangered themselves and their families. But, if they had learned later than this, they would have become so accustomed to pretending to be Christian that it would have been much harder for them to suddenly be Jewish.

The Origins of Bat Mitzvah

Starting in the second or third century of the Common Era, Jewish girls had a responsibility under Jewish law to observe *mitzvot* when they were twelve years old. Not until many centuries later, however, did families begin celebrating the girl's new status with some festivity.

By the 1800s, some families held a *seudat mitzvah* (a festive meal for a ritual occasion) on a girl's twelfth birthday. Sometimes the girl would deliver a talk at this meal.

Bat mitzvah has always been controversial among Orthodox Jews. Some believe that it should be a smaller celebration than bar mitzvah because girls must be more modest than boys. Others realize that girls should also learn Torah and that the custom of bat mitzvah therefore makes sense.

The first bat mitzvah ceremony in North America was that of the late Judith Kaplan Eisenstein, the daughter of Rabbi Mordecai Kaplan, the founder of the modern Jewish movement known as Reconstructionism. This happened in May 1922, when, as she later recalled, she was "midway between my twelfth and thirteenth birthdays."

Years later, she would remember that the night before the event, her father had still not decided on the exact form of the ceremony. The next day, as usual at a Shabbat service, Rabbi Kaplan read the *maftir* (the concluding portion of the Torah reading) and the *haftarah.* Then his daughter, "at a very respectable distance" from the Torah scroll (because girls traditionally did not read from the scroll), recited the first blessing and read the Torah selection from her own *chumash* (a book containing the Five Books of Moses).

As she later wrote, "The scroll was returned to the ark with song and procession, and the service was resumed. No thunder sounded, no lightning struck. The institution of bat mitzvah had been born without incident, and the rest of the day was all rejoicing."

In Reform Judaism and Reconstructionist Judaism, bar mitzvah and bat mitzvah are identical. In Conservative Judaism, practices range from the girl leading the service and reading from the Torah scroll to simply reading the *haftarah*. The time of the service might also vary. Some Conservative synagogues let a girl publicly celebrate becoming bat mitzvah on Shabbat morning. Others limit it to Friday evenings, or Monday, Thursday, and Rosh Chodesh (the first day of the Hebrew month) mornings when the Torah is also read in synagogue.

In mainstream Orthodoxy, the bat mitzvah ceremony basically consists of a sermonette on the Torah portion. This is followed by a festive meal. Sometimes the girl does the *devar Torah* (a sermonette on the Torah portion) in the sanctuary, sometimes in the social hall. Girls are seldom allowed to read directly from the Torah scroll. In some Orthodox synagogues, girls lead the service and read from either the Prophets or the Writings sections of the Bible. In Orthodoxy, bat mitzvah services may be held on Friday evening, Saturday evening, or Sunday morning, or even after the regular weekday morning service. Some Orthodox synagogues encourage girls to become bat mitzvah in a "women only" *minyan,* with the men watching from the outside! In England, some Orthodox Jewish girls become bat mitzvah in group ceremonies where they deliver scholarly speeches on topics of their choice.

Bar and Bat Mitzvah in Israel

Some families like to hold the bar and bat mitzvah ceremony in Israel. This is a wonderful idea, because it really helps create a firm bond with the Jewish state.

For many years, people have loved to have those ceremonies at the Western Wall. It is, after all, the most "traditional" place for the ceremony, and it has much historical and emotional power. But be aware: Girls cannot become bat mitzvah at the Wall. Not only this, but men and women must pray separately at the Wall. Increasingly, non-Orthodox Jews are taking their ceremonies to the southern part of the Wall, where there seems to be much less concern by the ultra-Orthodox about men and women praying together. Moreover, it is a beautiful site, overlooking the ancient city of David. For pure historical feeling, there is no better site.

People also like to have their ceremonies at the excavated synagogue at Masada, the palace built by King Herod, which overlooks the Dead Sea. This is where the last Jewish Zealots held out in the failed war of independence against the Romans in 73 C.E. Having a bar or bat mitzvah ceremony at Masada sends forth this message: *The Romans are gone, but we are still here. Judaism lives.*

Other people like to have their ceremonies at synagogues in Israel. Wherever you choose to have your ceremony in Israel, it sends a powerful message: *This is our land, and my moment of becoming a Jewish adult is linked to this land.*

What, Finally, Does It All Mean?

I believe that Jewish youngsters and their parents need to turn inward at bar and bat mitzvah time and ask themselves these hard questions: "Why are we doing this? What does it all mean?"

One thread links all the bar and bat mitzvah ceremonies throughout history, all the comings of age of every Jewish boy from Abraham on and of every Jewish girl from Sarah on. Bar and bat mitzvah means that you now are responsible for fulfilling the *mitzvot* of Jewish ritual. It is about growing up as a Jew. It is about becoming a fuller member of the Jewish community. It is about moral responsibility, about connecting to Torah, to community, to God.

★

What is your favorite definition
of bar or bat mitzvah? _____

If you could invent a Jewish rite of passage, what would it look like? What would be in it? Should there be a ritual for getting a driver's license?

_____

_____

What do you think of Judah ben Tema's
timeline for Jewish maturity?
How would you rewrite it? _____

_____

What should a Jewish kid be able to do
at thirteen? Fifteen? Eighteen? Twenty-one? _____

_____

What are some of the Jewish things that
you hope to do in the coming years? _____

Think about some of the *midrashim* on the age of thirteen. As a descendant of Abraham, what idols would you want to smash?

_____

As a descendant of Jacob, what choices are you going to be ready to
make when you become bar or bat mitzvah?

_____

As a descendant of Miriam, what are you willing to do to stand up for
Jewish survival? As a descendant of Bezalel,
what do you want to build in your life? _____

_____

If you were a Jewish parent in medieval Spain, how would you explain
Judaism to your thirteen-year-old son or daughter?

_____

Imagine that you, a Spanish Jewish teenager, have been given the
responsibility for telling a younger sibling that he or she is Jewish. What
would you say? What would you leave out?

_____

What would you like your parents to
know about how you feel about
becoming bar or bat mitzvah? _____

2

"Speak to the Children of Israel"

THE SECRET MEANING OF BAR AND BAT MITZVAH

*A generation can only receive the teachings in the sense that
it renews them. We do not take unless we also give.*

—Martin Buber

Some young people become *bar* or *bat* mitzvah. If you will forgive me for saying this, the greatest moment of my teenage years was *car* mitzvah.

I will never forget the day my father taught me how to drive on the local expressway. Back in those days, the speed limit was 65 mph—and I couldn't wait to get there! As I accelerated, the needle slowly moved up the speedometer. Suddenly, out of the silence, my father spoke.

"Jeff, let up on the gas a little bit. Let the car shift into high."

He seemed almost sad. Whether he knew it or not, my father was saying, "Jeff, slow down just a bit. Look out the right window. There's your old elementary school. How I remember your first day there. How I remember the day you finally taught yourself how to ride a two-wheel bicycle, the day you realized that you could simply pick up your feet and pedal on your own. Just two weeks ago, you were slowly driving around the side streets of our neighborhood. Now you're racing along the expressway. Soon you'll be going to college—and you'll be gone. Ease up on the gas. Don't grow up so fast. Don't let me age so fast."

At the moment the car hit 65, my father realized that I was no longer a little child—and he was no longer a young father. It was a true moment of passage.

That moment will always be with me. But my father and I never spoke about it.

He and I were not alone in our silence: *many* silences exist between parents and adolescents.

Consider the young boy in my synagogue who would be celebrating his bar mitzvah in three weeks. During his rehearsal in the sanctuary, I noted that his Hebrew—Torah, *haftarah* (the section from the Prophets), and prayers—was flawless. He was still working on his *devar Torah* (a sermonette on the Torah portion). He and his parents had neither discussed the meaning of the Torah portion nor read the translation of the Torah portion together. They were clueless.

"Have you and your parents discussed why you're becoming bar mitzvah?" I asked. There was silence.

"So," I prodded, trying to get a reaction. "Why are you doing this? Why are you becoming bar mitzvah?"

"It's what you do," he replied. "It's a tradition."

It was clear to me that he and his parents spent more time discussing which video to rent than discussing the deeper meaning behind bar mitzvah.

So, what do *bar* and *mitzvah* really mean?

"Don't Let Down the Coach"

In the *midrash* (*Kohelet Rabbah* 12:10), compiled in the eighth century C.E., we read: "The words of the wise are like a young girl's ball. As a ball is tossed by hand without falling, so Moses received the Torah at Sinai and delivered it to Joshua, Joshua to the elders, the elders to the prophets, and the prophets delivered it to the Great Synagogue." That is how the ancient rabbis imagined the *shalshelet ha-kabbalah,* "the great chain of tradition," that went from generation to generation: a ball that is tossed, playfully, from teacher to student. (By the way, who is throwing the ball? Not a boy, but a *girl.* The ancient rabbis knew that girls could make fine athletes!)

I once told a group of pre-teens that being Jewish means knowing about the Coach. Once, I said, at a place called Mount Sinai, the Coach gathered us together, saying, "OK, Cohen, Schwartz, Goldberg, even you, O'Malley (whose descendants will someday join the Jewish people through conversion). Here's the plan. Go out for the long pass. I throw the ball to you, you catch it, then throw it to your kids, who will throw it to their kids. That is how the ball gets passed from generation to generation."

The ball has gone from Israel to Spain to Germany to Poland to Russia to Northern Africa. We know the names of some of the ball throwers: Moses, Aaron, Deborah, David, Miriam, Ruth, Rabbi Akiba, Beruriah, Maimonides, and Henrietta Szold. Each of our ancestors had his or her own way of catching the ball, of running with it, and then throwing it. Certain generations fumbled the ball, and almost let it slip through their hands. But they never completely lost the ball.

Our generation won't drop the ball. If we do, there is no guarantee that it will bounce back again into our hands so we can throw it to future generations.

There are rules to this "game" of Judaism. *Number One:* Never forget that you are playing on a team that is larger than the people you see before you. It is a very, very big team. *Number Two:* Never let down your team members. You may not know them. If you do, you may not like some of them. But they need you, and you need them, for the ball to continue being passed through the generations. *Number Three: Never let down the Coach.*

Bar and bat mitzvah is a time when you get possession of the "ball." You must catch it, run with it well, and have enough knowledge and commitment to be able to throw it to your children, the next generation of ball throwers and ball catchers. It's the least we can do for God, for ourselves, and the Jewish future.

"Keep Up Your Part in the Choir"

For decades, a town in California traditionally began its monthly concerts with the singing of the "Star-Spangled Banner." One year, a guest conductor came to lead the orchestra. He wasn't familiar with the custom regarding the national anthem. As the opening bars of the first piece wafted through the auditorium, the audience realized that part of their tradition was missing.

Suddenly, a teenager rose and began singing the "Star-Spangled Banner." Slowly, others rose and also began singing. Soon, everyone was standing and everyone was singing. The singing was so powerful it drowned out the orchestra, which simply stopped playing. The musicians were dumbfounded. When the anthem was over, the orchestra applauded for the townspeople, for in many ways their performance was more exquisite than anything the professionals could have given.

We are all part of the Jewish community's "choir." The choir is made up of every Jew now alive, and every Jew who has ever lived and who *will* ever live. Every Jew has a piece of music with his or her part written upon it.

Some of you will be tempted to walk away from the choir. This is not good. We need you. Some Jews will have the music in their hands, but they will merely stand silent while the rest of the choir is singing. This is also not good, for we need their voices. Every voice is unique. Every voice has something powerful to add to this ancient melody of the Jewish people. Think of what would happen if every person in the choir decided not to sing. There would be silence. And we have labored too long at preserving our chorus of faith to let its message fall silent.

Some people will sing their part and then improvise a little bit. This is fine. Judaism is more like jazz or rock music than it is like classical music. Judaism means taking an ancient theme and improvising and even jamming on it. If we all sing our part, the result is a glorious harmony that can transform the world. Each of us has a voice. Each of us hears questions that are uniquely addressed to us: Where is your voice? What will you bring to our ancient melody?

"Don't Break the Chain!"

I once sat in my study with a girl who was debating whether to continue her Jewish education beyond the age of thirteen. She just wasn't sure. I asked her finally, "Have you ever received a chain letter? Not the kind that asks for money, but the kind that just asks you to pass on a message of peace or good will."

"Sure," she replied.

"How do you feel when you get a chain letter?"

"Actually, at first I feel pretty mad. After all, I didn't ask to get it."

"Right. What else is true about chain letters?"

"Well, there is usually some stuff in there about either good luck that comes to you if you continue the chain, or bad luck that happens to you if you break the chain."

"So, what do you do when you get a chain letter?"

"I usually sit down and send it on to five friends. Something bad could happen if I break the chain. Or, something good could happen if I *don't* break the chain."

"Exactly. But do you usually know the person who sent you the chain letter?"

"Well, sometimes . . ."

"Then why continue with the letter?"

She fidgeted a bit. "Well, I guess I feel a sense of responsibility..."

"You feel a sense of responsibility to people you don't even know and never met and may never meet. The Torah is like a chain letter. As with a chain letter, the process of passing it on has a lot of responsibility and a lot of power, and even a small amount of fear. Bad things could happen if we all crumpled up that 'chain letter' and simply dropped it into the wastebasket. Our people could cease to exist. But if you continue the chain, *great* things could happen to us and to our faith."

✦

What have your parents told you about bar or bat mitzvah?

_____

_____

What have your grandparents told you? What would you like to tell them about bar or bat mitzvah?

_____

_____

How would you explain bar or bat mitzvah to a non-Jewish friend? What stories, images, and ideas would you use?

_____

_____

Imagine yourself "getting the ball" of Judaism from someone. Who threw it to you? What will you do with it?

_____

_____

Think of a time when you have considered not "singing" your part in the "Judaism choir." What kept you singing anyway?

_____

_____

How is the Torah like a chain letter? _____

_____

What responsibility do you have to those who sent you the "chain letter of Torah"? _____

_____

_____

3

Why Are These People Crying?

WADING IN THE RIVER OF TEARS

May you live to see your world fulfilled
May your destiny be for worlds still to come
and may you trust in generations past and yet to be
May your heart be filled with intuition
and your words be filled with insight
May songs of praise ever be upon your tongue
and your vision be a straight path before you
May your eyes shine with the light of holy words
and your face reflect the brightness of the heavens . . .

—Talmud, *Berachot* 17a

There is no such thing as a bar or bat mitzvah ceremony without tears.

The tears may belong to several people. They belong to parents who are swelling with pride and relief. They belong to grandparents who may have come up to the *bimah* (the raised platform in synagogue, where the leader of the service stands) for their *aliyah* (blessing over the Torah). They listen to their grandchild read or chant from the Torah, and by the time they utter the closing blessing, their lips are trembling and their tears are falling. I have seen tears fall right onto the Torah scroll. Of all the places where tears might fall, that is the holiest place of all.

Let me tell you about the River of Tears. It is an ancient legend that I invented.

34

There is a River of Tears at every bar or bat mitzvah ceremony. Normally, tears are salty, but this River of Tears is sweet. This river flows with the tears of parents who have heard their children read from Torah. It is a very powerful river, for it is a very ancient river. It is a river that began in ancient Israel, and then flowed to Babylonia, and then to Spain and France and England, Germany and Poland and the United States, Canada, Australia, South Africa, Israel, and Argentina. It is a river that flows from generation to generation. It is a river that flows wherever our people has lived and worshiped. It gets mightier and sweeter with every passing Shabbat.

Why do people cry at bar and bat mitzvah ceremonies? And what can *you* learn from their tears?

We Feel That We Are Part of a Tribe

One of my favorite scenes in movie Westerns is the one in which an Indian chief takes his young son for a walk and says to him, "My son, it is time for you to learn our tribal wisdom."

We Jews are also a tribe—a tribe that is melded together out of the descendants of the original Twelve Tribes of Israel. The Torah is our tribal wisdom.

Throughout history, we have lived in exile from our homeland in the land of Israel. But, as the nineteenth-century German Jewish poet Heinrich Heine said, the Torah has been our portable homeland. Even when we were strangers living in strange lands, when we learned Torah it was like being at home again. Recently in synagogue, a boy who was becoming bar mitzvah was holding the Torah scroll. This is what he said: "It feels like holding a big teddy bear." Just as holding a teddy bear can give us a feeling of security, the Torah also makes us feel safe.

One of the most remarkable religious leaders of the twenty-first century is the Dalai Lama, the spiritual leader of Tibet. He is remarkable for many reasons, but mainly because he has done such a wonderful job of keeping his people together, even though the government of China has done so much to destroy the religious and cultural life of Tibet.

A few years ago, the Dalai Lama met with Jewish leaders and

teachers. He had one main question for them: "How have you managed to live for so long in exile from your homeland?" He hoped the answer would guide and inspire him as he led Tibetans who were in exile from their own country.

Our teachers told him this: When you go on a trip, there are certain things that you pack with you. On our long "trip," in our wandering throughout the centuries, we Jews put some very valuable things into our "backpacks." We brought our values (such as righteousness, mercy, compassion, justice), our holy books (such as the Torah and the Talmud), and our ideas and ideals about the family.

When we celebrate the sacred moments of life, like bar and bat mitzvah, we feel the tug of those things that are familiar to us. We feel as if we are "home." A Protestant teacher, Archie Smith, once defined worship as the act of forgetting that you've forgotten. That is one reason for worship. Whenever we pray together, we forget that we have forgotten our Jewish roots. We suddenly remember. We have come "home." (In computer terms, it's as if we have suddenly realized that the hard drive really did not crash after all—that all the data are there just where we left them. We just have to figure out how to access the data.)

That is why some people cry at bar and bat mitzvah ceremonies. They may not realize it, but they are saying to themselves: "So many things in life are unfamiliar. So many things in life change all the time. I've been living in my house for, say, twelve years. In the greater scheme of things, that's a relatively short time. But there is something that goes beyond me, and that's the Torah. And this young person whom I love is now reading the Torah publicly for the first time. Hearing that, I feel as if I am really home."

So bar and bat mitzvah reminds us who we are as Jews. Just think: You could celebrate your thirteenth birthday by taking ten of your friends to a football game or to the theater. Instead, you read Torah, because it is our "tribal wisdom." And when you do that, you feel as if you are home.

It is a very good feeling.

We Feel a Sense of Immortality

A Jewish playwright, Donald Margulies, wrote a play a few years ago called *The Loman Family Picnic*. In the play, a family is getting ready for the oldest son's bar mitzvah. At the party, the mother "sees" and waves to invisible guests: family members who died in the Holocaust.

Scary, yes. But this is not like *Tales from the Crypt*. It is good, serious Judaism. Many Jewish rituals require that you imagine yourself as *someone else* or that *invisible guests* are with you.

Consider this: At the Passover seder, we imagine that we are slaves leaving Egypt. (Some Jews actually act out the Exodus during their seder.) At a Jewish wedding, the bride and groom imagine that they are the first couple, Adam and Eve, in the Garden of Eden.

On Sukkot, the harvest festival, we imagine that the great Jews of the Bible "visit" our *sukkah*. In the Bible (2 Kings 2:1–11), the prophet Elijah seems not to have died. Instead, he is swept up into the heavens in a chariot of fire—and so, the ancient rabbis imagined that Elijah never really died. To this day, he has some tasks to perform. Elijah "visits" every *brit milah* (the ritual circumcision ceremony), ensuring that the covenant still lives. Because Elijah is supposed to announce the coming of the Messiah, he also makes a "guest appearance" at the seder, because if we are lucky, the Messiah might come that very night!

At every life-cycle event, something remarkable happens. There is a reunion between the living and the dead. As the great Jewish scholar Rabbi Jacob Neusner has said, "At a bar or a bat mitzvah, a parent thinks not so much of the future as of the past, especially if a grandparent or a parent is deceased."

For that reason, bar and bat mitzvah ceremonies are far more "crowded" than anyone can imagine. The visible and the invisible generations are present, just as they were present for the sealing of the covenant at Mount Sinai approximately three thousand years ago.

I remember a particular bat mitzvah in my last congregation. The father of the bat mitzvah came up to the Torah for his *aliyah* and started weeping almost uncontrollably.

"My father and my brother are both dead," he told me later. "My kids are named for both of them. And now my daughters are both mature Jewish adults. I felt that the cycle was complete. Times like that make me think there really is a God in the world. It's remembering people who have died. I could almost hear them taking pleasure in my daughter reading the Torah."

Life cycle events have a way of reminding us that our loved ones are immortal. What is the piece of us that is immortal? It is called the *soul.* No one has ever seen a soul, but it is the essence of who we are, the invisible spark that makes us *us.* Every human being has a soul. Our people have a soul as well: the Torah. When we share moments of Torah, we guarantee that our people will live forever.

The prophet Ezekiel had a vision of a valley of dry bones—the Jewish people after the destruction of Jerusalem in 586 B.C.E.—miraculously coming back to life. It wasn't such a crazy vision. We modern Jews, too, have seen dry bones come back to life. We live more than sixty years after the Holocaust. And so, whenever Jewish parents and grandparents see the children they love becoming bar and bat mitzvah, it reminds them: I am not the last Jew on earth. Whenever the Torah is read, it cries out to us: The Jewish people lives. When we read the Torah, we guarantee our immortality as a people.

Sometimes parents and children see how they are connected to Jewish history. Bonnie was about to become the first bat mitzvah in her family's history. Her grandparents were Holocaust survivors, and her mother had been born in a displaced persons' camp in Germany.

As Bonnie and I were discussing the more mundane aspects of the ceremony, her mother noted, "There won't be many people there. Actually, there will be more from my husband's side than from mine." A silence fell upon us. Most of her "side" had disappeared in the death camps.

I said to Bonnie, "Along with all the other important reasons for becoming bat mitzvah, there is another reason. When you stand on the *bimah* in the synagogue that morning, you will be spitting in Hitler's face."

It was my own restatement of the words of the philosopher Emil Fackenheim. Fackenheim said that since the Holocaust, the Jewish people have had an additional commandment: Don't let Hitler win!

Judaism lives—through Bonnie, her family, and their faith, and through the faith of every Jew alive today.

Parents Feel They Are Getting Older

Your parents may not want to believe this, but they are now thirteen years older than they were when you were born. There is simply no way of getting out of that.

As we said in the first chapter, bar mitzvah may be related to the *brit milah* (ritual circumcision) ceremony that occurs when a boy is eight days old. At that ceremony, the parent says, "As we have brought this child into the covenant of Abraham, so, too, will he be brought into the study of Torah, the *chupah* [the wedding canopy], and the performance of good deeds." Bar mitzvah therefore, is the occasion when the community sees that the parent has fulfilled the first part of the promise. Ideally, the same people who attended the *brit* will also be present when the young person becomes bar mitzvah.

Of course, today we would include baby-namings for girls and prayers by mothers in this spiritual inheritance. You may think that bar and bat mitzvah is *your* passage. But guess what? Parents need rites of passage as much as their children do.

This is what might be happening in your parents' heads: "I am now entering middle age. Do I still have what it takes to be successful in life? Am I still being creative? How am I doing in my career? How am I doing as a parent? How am I doing as a son or daughter to my own parents?"

Or: "Uh-oh, now I'm *really* a grownup! Thirteen years ago, at the *brit milah* (or the baby-naming), my parents did me a favor. They ordered the deli platters for the meal. But now I have to make all the plans for the bar (or bat) mitzvah celebration. It's on my shoulders now. And that little kid, the one I promised to make a Jew—this is it. I said that I would bring this child to the study of Torah. So, how much Torah does this child *really* know? Is our tradition safe in his (or her) hands? Have I done my job well? This is the big test—for all of us."

But here's something else that is nice about Judaism. It can guide us through our passages. It can say to us: "Don't worry about how old you are or how young you are. There are *mitzvot* to do and there is Torah to learn. Don't worry. When you act like a Jew, you realize that all life really does have meaning."

Grandparents Sense Their Own Aging

When grandparents bless the Torah at their grandchild's bar or bat mitzvah, they are often aware of many things. They remember their own parents, which often means that they remember their own Jewish coming-of-age. They remember what it was like fifty, sixty, maybe seventy years before, when they were thirteen and their parents and grandparents stood over them at their own bar mitzvah. Many, if not most, of the grandmothers will not have those memories of becoming bat mitzvah. It doesn't matter. They still feel the presence of their own parents and grandparents.

Your grandparents feel that the years are flying by. They are not young any more. Neither are your parents, their own children. As grandparents look into the evening of their lives, they realize that they may be less vibrant than before and that their own generation is no longer in charge.

But bar and bat mitzvah does something beautiful, even for your grandparents. It makes getting older easier on them. The Talmud teaches this: When you hear your grandchild reading Torah, it is like hearing the words from Sinai itself. Grandparents, even those who call themselves "unreligious," cry when their grandchildren read Torah. They sense that their grandchildren are speaking words from Sinai, words that their own grandparents might have said to them, words that have kept us, the Jewish people, alive for centuries and centuries.

Why is bar and bat mitzvah so popular? And what's the secret reason why your family is looking forward to your ceremony? Because at this particular ceremony, you represent all of Judaism: Jewish triumphs, tragedies, wisdom, virtues, and hopes. You are now a constant reminder of Jewish yesterdays that were fulfilled or frustrated, and of Jewish tomorrows still to come.

✦

What is your secret of Jewish survival?
What has kept us alive over the centuries?_____

_____

Talk to your parents about their feelings as you prepare to become bar or bat mitzvah. What are they feeling? How does this compare with your feelings? _____

_____

What are the things in Judaism that make you feel most secure?

_____

Have you ever felt the "presence" of departed relatives? What kinds of occasions bring those presences to mind?

_____

What things can you do to make sure that Hitler did not succeed in destroying Judaism and the Jewish people?

_____

✶

Interview your parents and grandparents about their bar and bat mitzvah experiences. Ask them:

Where were you bar or bat mitzvah? What was the name of the synagogue? What kind of synagogue was it?

_____

How did you prepare to become bar or bat mitzvah? Did you go to Hebrew school? Did you have a special tutor?

_____

_____

_____

Who was the rabbi? The cantor? What were the names of your teachers? (These names should never be lost. They are important people in Jewish history—because without them, you would not be becoming bar or bat mitzvah!)_____

_____

What did it mean to you to become a bar or bat mitzvah?

_____

_____

What does it mean to you when you say "I am Jewish"?

_____

_____

What did you like best about the process? The least?

_____

_____

What was your Torah portion? Did you give a _devar Torah_? What do you remember about it?

_____

_____

How did your parents participate? _____

_____

What was the celebration like? Who planned it? What was served at it? Was there music? Dancing?

_____

_____

Did you continue your Jewish education after becoming bar or bat mitzvah? Why or why not?

_____

If your parents or grandparents did not have bar or bat mitzvah ceremonies, why not? Do they ever wish that they had?

_____

_____

4

Hearing God's Voice

THE MEANING OF TORAH

The divine word spoke to each and every person according to his or her particular capacity: the young according to their capacity, the old in keeping with their capacity . . .

—Midrash, *Pesikta de Rav Kahana*

Something uplifting and holy occurs when you read from the Torah scroll on the day when you become bar or bat mitzvah. You may not even notice it at the time, but it is happening and it is real. This occurs because the Torah is at the very center of our faith. It is our story, our vision, our sense of ourselves, the most basic record of what God wants of us.

Torah has several meanings. It literally means "teaching." But when we speak about reading from *the* Torah, we mean reading from the *sefer Torah,* the Torah scroll itself. As you probably know, the scroll contains the Five Books of Moses. These are the books that Jews have traditionally said that Moses received from God at Sinai. Each book has a Greek or an English name, and also a Hebrew name, which corresponds to the first or second words of the book. Therefore, Genesis, the Greek name, is *Bereshit* ("When God began to create") in Hebrew. Exodus is *Shemot* ("These are the names"); Leviticus is *Vayikra* ("And

God called"); Numbers is *Bemidbar* ("In the wilderness"); and Deuteronomy is *Devarim* ("The words").

What Torah Portion Will You Read?

It takes a full year of the Jewish calendar, starting in the fall with the Festival of Simchat Torah, to read the entire Torah. You will read (or chant, according to the custom of your synagogue) the *parashah,* the Torah portion for that particular week. This is also called the *sedra.*

If your thirteenth birthday falls roughly between October and the end of December, you will probably read from *Bereshit,* or Genesis, which spans the years from Creation to Joseph's death in Egypt. Much of the Bible's best stories are in Genesis: Creation, Cain and Abel, Noah and the Flood, and the tales of the patriarchs and matriarchs, Abraham, Isaac, Jacob, Sarah, Rebeccah, and Leah. It also includes one of the greatest pieces of literature in history, the story of Joseph, which takes up more than one-quarter of all of the book of Genesis.

If you become thirteen between January and the end of February, you will probably read a section from *Shemot,* or Exodus. This tells of our ancestors' slavery in Egypt, the rise of Moses and the Israelites' liberation from slavery, the parting of the Sea of Reeds (a better translation than the traditional "Red Sea," and besides, scholars are simply not sure which body of water the Israelites crossed), the giving of the Ten Commandments, the idolatry of the Golden Calf, and the design and construction of the Tabernacle, the sanctuary for the original tablets of the Law, which our ancestors carried with them in the desert. Exodus also includes various ethical and civil laws, such as "Don't wrong a stranger or oppress him, for you were strangers in the land of Egypt."

If you turn thirteen between early March and the end of May, you will probably read a section called *Vayikra,* or Leviticus. The book contains the laws of sacrifice and purity and other Temple rituals, which were the responsibility of the tribe of Levi, one of the twelve tribes of Israel.

If you become bar or bat mitzvah during the late spring or early summer (June or July), you will probably read *Bemidbar,* or Numbers, which describes the forty years of wandering in the wilderness and the various rebellions against Moses.

With August and the end of summer comes the end of the yearly reading of the Torah. *Devarim,* or Deuteronomy, the last book in the Torah, is Moses' farewell address to the Israelites as they prepare to enter the land of Israel. Various laws that were previously discussed are repeated, sometimes with different wordings. Deuteronomy ends with the death of Moses on Mount Nebo as he looks across the Jordan Valley into the land that he would not enter. Moses' great temper—hitting a rock rather than speaking to it in order to get water (Numbers 20:7–13)—kept him from entering the land of Israel. On Simchat Torah, we go from reading about the death of Moses at the end of the *sefer Torah* to reading about the creation of the world, at the beginning of the Torah scroll, without missing a beat.

What Else Is Torah?

The first part of the Jewish Bible is the Torah. But there is much more to it than these five books. The accurate term for the Jewish Bible is the *Tanach:* an abbreviation for *Torah, Neviim* (the Prophets, including Isaiah, Amos, Ezekiel, and Jeremiah, and books about early Israelite history like Joshua, Judges, Samuel, and Kings) and *Ketuvim* (the Writings such as Psalms, Song of Songs, Job, and Proverbs). In Hebrew, the Torah is also referred to as the *chumash;* in Greek, it is known as the *Pentateuch.* Both terms are derived from the word for "five" in their respective languages, because there are five books in the Torah.

In the broadest sense, Torah means not only studying the Torah (the *chumash,* the first five books of the Bible, the *Pentateuch,* the Scroll), but also studying the entire Hebrew Bible as well as studying later Jewish law and lore, such as the Mishnah, the Talmud, and the *midrash;* medieval Jewish Torah commentary, philosophy, poetry, and mysticism; Hasidism; and the teachings of modern Jewish scholars and philosophers. Torah means *everything* that we Jews have thought about, struggled with, and created during our history. So in a sense, when we say "Torah" we mean Judaism. We mean anything that emerges out of our study of Torah.

Torah continues into our own day. As *Pirke Avot* (the ethical teachings of the ancient rabbis) says, "Every day a voice goes forth from Sinai"—every day, at least, if we turn down the noise of the world and train our ears to hear the truth and the beauty of the Torah.

Judaism, then, is not just the words of the written Torah. It includes oral traditions that have been passed down over the generations. Jewish practices have changed since biblical days. For instance, we Jews no longer celebrate Passover by sacrificing a lamb. The Torah tells us not to work on the Sabbath and on the sacred days of the major holidays, like Yom Kippur, Sukkot, and Pesach. Yet, it never defines work. Rituals that now seem essential to Shabbat—candle lighting and *kiddush*—are nowhere in the Torah. *Kippah* (or *yarmulke*), the traditional Jewish ritual head coverings, are not in the Torah. The Torah does not mention several holidays that we now think are essential to Judaism, such as Chanukah and Purim. And it did not imagine the horrors of the Holocaust and the wondrous rebirth of the Jewish state of Israel, both of which have become central to how we modern Jews understand ourselves and our faith and our place in the world.

Judaism begins with *the* Torah. But ideally, Torah can become the way you view yourself as a Jew.

Just think about how the stories of Torah make a difference in our lives. Parents and children shudder when they hear about how Abraham almost sacrificed his son Isaac on Mount Moriah, because they think of how fragile life is, and what it means to sacrifice what we love the most. Every Jew who has become successful in a predominantly non-Jewish culture (like the United States, or England, or Canada, or almost anywhere in the world except Israel) can imagine what Joseph experienced in Egypt as he rose to the very top of Egyptian power. Every person who works for freedom and justice is with Moses at Pharaoh's court, yelling, "Let my people go!" Every teacher, leader, or politician can relate to Moses' frustrations in leading the Jewish people through the wilderness. Many aged persons who hear the tale of the death of Moses sigh when they think about what it might mean to die before reaching their most cherished goals.

The modern German Jewish thinkers Martin Buber and Franz

Rosenzweig translated the Hebrew word for Hebrew Bible, *mikra,* as "calling out." They knew that the Torah and the entire Hebrew Bible call out to each of us. If we listen carefully enough, we, too, will hear the call.

Some of those stories have our names upon them.

The *Haftarah:* The Rest of God's Call to Us

After you read or chant the Torah in the synagogue, you will read or chant the *haftarah,* which literally means "the conclusion." The *haftarah* portion comes from the *Neviim,* the Prophetic books, which are the second part of the Bible. It is either read or chanted from a Hebrew Bible, or you might read the appropriate passage from the *Neviim* from a booklet or a photocopy.

We read the Torah in the order of the books, from Creation at the beginning of Genesis to the death of Moses at the end of Deuteronomy. But the *haftarah* passages were chosen because their themes are connected to the Torah text. Sometimes, just a single word is enough to connect a *haftarah* to a Torah portion. They are not in any particular sequence.

Not all books in the Prophetic section of the Hebrew Bible consist of prophecy. Several are historical. The book of Joshua tells the story of the conquest and settlement of Israel. The book of Judges speaks of early tribal rulers when "no king ruled in Israel." Some judges are well known: Deborah, the great prophetess and military leader, and Samson, the great biblical strong man.

The books of Samuel start with Samuel, the last judge, and then move to the monarchy under Saul and David (approximately 1000 B.C.E.). The books of Kings tell of the death of King David, the rise of King Solomon, and how the Israelite kingdom split into the northern kingdom of Israel and the southern kingdom of Judah (approximately 900 B.C.E.).

What's special about these books? They show that the ancient Israelites were a rather *normal* people. We Jews were not a kingdom of holy people—at least, not yet. Our kings and generals were regular people who had real-life urges, failures, weaknesses, and triumphs. They were remarkably like us, and like our heroes and leaders in America today.

But many *haftarah* selections do contain the words of the prophets, those spokesmen for God whose words fired the Jewish conscience. Their names are immortal: Isaiah, Jeremiah, Ezekiel, Amos, Hosea. They spared no one their denunciations and criticisms. They taught that God commands us to behave decently toward one another, that God chose us *not* for special privileges but for special duties to humanity, that someday there will be universal justice and peace, that history is moving forward toward an ultimate conclusion that some call the Messianic Age: a time of universal peace and prosperity for the Jewish people and for all the people of the world.

Who are some modern prophets? A short list: the late Reverend Martin Luther King Jr.; Nelson Mandela and Archbishop Desmond Tutu, who fight for racial equality in South Africa; the late Rabbi Abraham Joshua Heschel, who spoke out about poverty and unjust wars; Elie Wiesel, the Holocaust survivor who reminds everyone about the dangers of hatred. The former United States Surgeon General Dr. C. Everett Koop acted like a prophet when he told us about the problems of AIDS and smoking. The late Rabbi Marshall Meyer was like a prophet, giving hope to those who were persecuted in Argentina in the 1970s. The late Israeli prime minister Yitzhak Rabin was like a prophet, because he fought valiantly for peace. And there are probably a lot of minor, almost anonymous prophets who go about their daily lives doing wonderful things that no one talks about. But they are there.

Here's the interesting thing about the *haftarot*. Many selections depict individual prophets criticizing the Jewish people. Well and good—that is what a prophet was *supposed* to do. But by the time each selection ends, the prophet speaks words of encouragement and comfort. Things *can* get better, the prophets say. Even though you may have blown it, you can do better. That, too, is a Jewish way of looking at the world. Every prophetic message ends on an optimistic note.

What a wonderful vision for the world.

Why You Read Torah

I once asked some parents of candidates for bar and bat mitzvah, "What does it mean for your child to read Torah when he or she becomes bar or bat mitzvah?" Among their responses:

✦ "It means that my son has completed his studies and achieved his goal that was taught in Hebrew and Sunday school."

✦ "It signifies that she has come of age in the Jewish religion."

✦ "He learns values from the Torah that can be applied to real life."

✦ "A link with his ancestors in a common bond that dates back for thousands of years."

✦ "A special moment in her life to read from such a special and sacred scroll."

I was disappointed. One small word was missing from all their descriptions. What makes this act of learning, reading, and interpreting Torah *different* from all your other experiences? One thing: *God*.

Let's face it: we modern Jews don't like to speak about God. Oh, we might talk about feeling God's presence in nature or when we have lost someone we love. Sometimes when we are struggling with an ethical decision, we might say that the "still, quiet voice" spoke to us, sort of like Jiminy Cricket in *Pinocchio*.

We get nervous talking about the relationship between God and Torah because if we started really thinking about it we might conclude that God *wrote* the Torah. And if God wrote the Torah, how dare we disagree with any of it? And if God wrote the Torah, what do we do with those things in the Torah that make us uncomfortable? I believe that God is part of the experience of reading Torah—that you can't read the Torah without thinking about God. That means that we encounter God whenever we read or study Torah. But reading Torah has always meant that people of every generation have a chance to interpret it so that it means something special to them.

Consider the following famous legend from the Talmud. At one level, this is about the great second-century sage Rabbi Akiva. But at a deeper level, it tells us that Torah is truly timeless.

> When Moses ascended Sinai, he found God attaching little crowns to the letters of the Torah.
>
> "Master of the Universe," asked Moses, "why are You attaching these crowns to the Torah?"
>
> "Someday in the future," replied God, "a man will appear named Akiva ben Joseph. He will be able to come up with all sorts of interpretations based on these little crowns."
>
> "Let me see him," said Moses.
>
> "Turn around," said God.
>
> Moses was transported to a class in Akiva's academy. But he could not understand what was going on, and he was distressed.
>
> Finally, a certain subject came up and the students asked Akiva, "How do you know this?" and Akiva replied, "This is a teaching from Moses on Sinai." And Moses was pleased."
>
> —Talmud, *Menahot* 29b

Akiva could find the echoes of what Moses heard on Sinai in what he was teaching. If we can properly train our ears, so can we. Here's the big challenge: Can you link becoming bar or bat mitzvah to the moment when Moses received the tablets at Sinai? Can you interpret on your own what you find in the Torah? When you do, you will feel that you, like Moses, are standing at the top of your own "Mount Sinai." You will also discover something amazing. The Torah scroll is written without vowels, which means that the Torah as we have it in the scroll is only *partially complete.* When you read it and interpret it, the words become "real." You fill in the vowels, and the words become your words. By the time you are done, the scroll will have your name on it.

So Where Is God's Presence in the Scroll?

"Come on, rabbi," a woman recently said to me. "This stuff about God and the Torah—I don't get it. Isn't the Torah just great literature?"

Well, yes, it is. Most of it, anyway. But let's admit it: some material in the Torah isn't great literature. Consider the lists of "begats" (the genealogical lists of who fathered which child) in Genesis, the first book of the Bible. Is *this* great literature? How about the long list of Edomite kings (the descendants of Jacob's twin brother, Esau) in the book of Genesis? Is *this* great literature? Hardly. However, a mystical teacher said that someday we will find that there is a hidden meaning to even the list of kings. Wisdom can turn up in strange, unlikely places. I'm waiting for that "someday." But it hasn't happened yet.

Is the Torah *only* great literature? Is that *really* its hold upon us? Think of William Shakespeare, the great English writer. His works are among the greatest in the history of the world. I love going to a theater to see Shakespeare's play *Hamlet*. But when I do go, I don't expect that seeing it will make me into a better or holier person.

If a copy of *Hamlet* were in a burning building, no modern Englishman would run into that building to save the book from the fire. But that is precisely what generations of Jews have done for the Torah scroll. If we were to look at the Torah as simply the great literature of our people, then it would not command us or move us as it does, and as it has for many generations.

The Torah scroll makes us think of Jewish history and Jewish tradition in a way that no other Jewish ritual object can. By touching something deep inside of us, it affects us as few other things can.

How do we know that God is somehow involved in Torah? The way we act toward the Torah scroll is all the evidence you need.

Here is a small lesson in *halachah,* traditional Jewish law. A person who accidentally drops a Torah scroll must atone by fasting or giving to charity. Some say whoever witnesses the dropping of the Torah must also fast as an act of mourning. Why? Because the Torah symbolizes the possibility that God *really* spoke to our ancestors, really inspired them, really gave them the ability to create stories and laws that they believed reflected the Divine Will.

You may treat that scroll only with total reverence and respect. This is why the Nazis delighted in damaging Torah scrolls and transforming them into such objects as shoes and even a banjo. On *Kristallnacht* in November 1938, the "Night of Broken Glass" when Jewish homes, businesses, and synagogues in Germany were destroyed, anti-Semitic thugs unraveled Torah scrolls out of synagogue windows. The Nazis had declared war not only on the Jews and not only on Judaism—they had declared war on God. And they attacked the Torah scrolls knowing that those scrolls symbolized God.

On that night, Jews ran back into their burning synagogues to rescue Torah scrolls. They *all* felt the pull of the scroll, the same pull felt by each generation of Jews dating back to Sinai.

How Do We Experience God in the Service?

The high moment of Shabbat morning worship is the Torah service. The emotional "center" of that service occurs when the Torah is removed from the *aron hakodesh,* the Holy Ark.

What is the Ark? And what does it mean to us?

The Ark reminds us of the Holy of Holies in the ancient Temple in Jerusalem. That was where the tablets that Moses received on Sinai were kept. According to some Jewish traditions, the Holy of Holies was located on a very sacred spot. It was the place, they say, where Adam was born, and where Noah made his offering to God after the flood, and where Abraham bound Isaac as a sacrifice to God, and where Jacob dreamed of a ladder of angels. Moslems say it is where Mohammed ascended to heaven. Jewish tradition believes that is the sacred center of the world.

On the ninth day of the Hebrew month of Av in the year 70 C.E., the Romans destroyed the Temple as the crushing blow in their war against the Jews. Ever since, we Jews have lacked this sacred geographic and spiritual center. But three times a week, or whenever the Torah is read—Monday, Thursday, Shabbat morning and afternoon, and festival mornings—we "forget" that the center has been destroyed. We go before the Ark, the holiest spot in the holiest area in the holiest room in the holiest building that we know. And there, something "magical" happens.

Then the Ark in the synagogue is no longer "just" the Ark in our synagogue. Suddenly, it "becomes" the Ark in the ancient Temple in Jerusalem. When the Torah is taken out to be read, suddenly something happens to us. We are no longer modern Jews. We "become" very ancient Jews, and we feel as if we were standing at Mount Sinai when God gave the Torah to Moses.

So imagine that when you take the scroll out of the Ark as you become bar or bat mitzvah, you will re-create the giving of the Torah to Moses. You will "be" Moses. And the people in the congregation, sitting in front of you, are no longer just your friends and relatives and members of the community. They "are" the ancient Israelites at the foot of Mount Sinai. At that moment, we are one with all Jews who have ever lived, who are living now, and who ever will live. Maybe the synagogue is only half full. But don't believe it. It is as though every Jew who has ever lived, who is living now, and who ever will live is present.

It's true: you need a very powerful imagination to be Jewish. Imagine if someone suggested that you read or chant the Torah portion from a printed page or even from a bound book. Forget about it. The Scroll itself has something magical about it as well. It is our connection to the God who loves us and who made and keeps a covenant, a sacred relationship, with us.

Did God Write the Torah?

It depends on whom you ask.

Orthodox Jews believe that God gave the Divine Word to Moses at Sinai. The Divine Word took two forms: the written Torah *(Torah she-bichtav)* and the oral *Torah (Torah she-be-al peh),* which was ultimately written down as the Mishnah and the Talmud. For Orthodox Jews, the oral tradition is the official interpretation of the written Torah.

Conservative Jews have many different ideas about God's role in giving Torah. Some Conservative thinkers, such as the very influential rabbi Abraham Joshua Heschel, who died in 1972, say that God did reveal the Divine Word at Sinai, but that these revelations were transcribed by human beings. That is why there are often contradictions in the Bible. For instance, one version of the Creation story says that Adam and Eve were created by God at the same time; another version says that Eve was created after Adam was created, and she was made out of Adam's side. This Conservative idea of Torah's history is a lot like playing "telephone"—the message may have started out right, but it can get garbled over time.

Other Conservative thinkers say that people wrote down the Torah, but that they were divinely inspired. Still others say that Torah is the record of the encounter between God and the Jewish people at Sinai. Since that record was written by human beings, it contains some laws and ideas that we might reject as being old-fashioned and even hopelessly out of date, like teachings that seem to put down women.

In general, Conservative Judaism believes in *conserving* much of the traditional view of Torah. Conservative Judaism sees that our understanding of the Torah is affected by the *time* in which we live and *how* we live our lives. It honors tradition while keeping today's realities in mind.

Then, there is Reconstructionist Judaism. Reconstructionist Judaism was developed by one of the more extraordinary Jews of the twentieth century, Rabbi Mordecai Kaplan, who lived from 1881 to 1983. Reconstructionists believe that the Torah is the sacred record of our people's search for God. We are therefore not only descendants who receive Torah, but ancestors that help interpret and shape Torah for another generation.

There is the approach of Reform Judaism, which believes that Torah results from the relationship between God and the Jewish people. That relationship is very ancient, and it continues to unfold in every age. Therefore, the process of the giving of Torah is unfolding. In the words of Professor Michael Meyer of Hebrew Union College–Jewish Institute of Religion:

> The Torah is not for me divine revelation in any literal sense. Rather the Pentateuch [the five books of Moses], the Prophets, the Writings, and the rabbinic literature represent our people's ongoing historical endeavor to verbalize their experience of a God who represents the objective reality of justice, mercy, and love.

Finally, what do I believe about Torah? I believe that God and the Jewish people met at Mount Sinai. It was very hard to put that experience into words, but as our sages and teachers thought about that encounter and what it meant, they put those thoughts into words, and the words became Torah. What they did is like listening to a concert recording. No matter how good that recording is, it can never completely reproduce the feeling of the live concert. Yet, it is all we have.

In the same way, the Torah is our "recording" of what happened at Sinai. It is far from being a perfect record of that moment. But it is still our closest understanding of how God wants us to live. And every time we study it, it is as if God speaks to us again.

Can We "Hear" God in the Torah? Sometimes It Is Very Easy

There are certainly moments when I imagine that I "hear" the authentic voice of God in the Torah.

What can compare with the opening words of the scroll: *Bereshit bara Elohim* ("When God began to create heaven and earth")? This is precisely *not* the time to start worrying about geology and physics and the real age of the earth. The opening words of Genesis teach us that there is order and meaning in the world. Since God made the world, *Bereshit* suggests that we who are made in God's image must guard what God created. And since God included rest in the order of creation, *Bereshit* tells us that Shabbat is holy.

The Torah has many other stories about God's presence: Abraham setting forth at God's command to a land that he did not yet know; the revelation of the Ten Commandments; Moses dying in solitude on Mount Nebo, overlooking the Land of Israel.

Why is God in those stories? Because they have an overwhelming beauty. Because of the emotions they inspire. And most often, because their values have survived into our time. When you interpret those stories and decide how their values speak to you, *that* is God's voice you'll be hearing. It may sound like your voice, but God will be there, whispering to you and encouraging you.

When the stories of Torah really become *our* stories, it is a remarkable moment. A few years ago, I taught Marcie, a twelve-year-old girl, the story in the Midrash of how Miriam, the sister of Moses, prevailed upon her parents to maintain their marital relationship, even amid the stress of the oppression of Jews in Egypt. As a result, Marcie convinced her own parents, who were having some serious problems, to make up and stay together. Marcie had found her own story, her own life, and her own struggle in the scroll, and that story told her what to do.

Sometimes it is very hard to hear God speaking to us from a book. But if we try, we can hear God telling us to strive for inspiration. There might even be a jewel in that story or book. Take, for example, the stories in Exodus of the building of the Tabernacle, the ancient portable worship place that our ancestors carried through the wilderness after fleeing slavery in Egypt. The stories of the building of the Tabernacle remind us that everyone had a hand in that sacred project; and therefore, all Jews are potentially holy and have holy tasks to do. They tell us that the Tabernacle was made up of pieces that all fit together perfectly, and that if we strive for wisdom and holiness, all of the "pieces" of our lives fit together as well. Finally, the accounts of the building of the Tabernacle remind us that *religion needs a central place in which to occur.* In this way, it is not different from sports. You can't play baseball without a baseball diamond. When people ask, "But do you really need a synagogue to be Jewish?" I like to answer, "But do you really need a stadium to be a baseball fan? Do you really need a concert hall to love live music? Do you really need a stage to be a dancer?"

What about Leviticus? Leviticus is a tough book. Most of it is concerned with ritual laws, and many of them are about difficult subjects: sacrifices, blood, altars, purity, and impurity.

What can we learn from the laws of sacrifice today when we don't sacrifice anything? Simply this: Sacrifice is about being grateful. A long time ago, to demonstrate their gratitude, Jews brought to a holy place their most valuable possession: the first and best of their flocks. If you think about it a bit, this isn't strange. Try this experiment: Tear a twenty-dollar bill into little pieces. Go ahead—I dare you! It's hard to do it. Why? Because it is valuable. For ancient Israelites to bring their best animals to be sacrificed was a way of saying: "I am very small. But you, God, are bigger than everything. I must give you something that is precious."

This idea is more modern than you think. Sometimes store owners frame the first dollar bill they ever earned as a symbol of gratitude for their success. Sacrifice teaches us that religion, like life, is not a free ride. It takes commitment. It requires giving a piece of yourself to God.

And then there's the portion in Leviticus known as *Tazria,* which is sometimes combined with another portion, *Metzora.* It is not exactly the most delightful material in the Torah: a woman is ritually impure after childbirth. There is a detailed description of a skin disease that may be leprosy or psoriasis, in which there are irritating skin rashes.

And yet, the best bar and bat mitzvah speeches of the year are always about this portion.

What is there to say about psoriasis, an irritating skin disease? The Torah tells us that the disease caused a great deal of social fear, just like AIDS, cancer, and epilepsy today. In our time, illness still creates great fear. People are afraid of the unknown and they are scared of people who look different.

When young people make the connection between how we are afraid of illness and how words of Torah can help us heal, Torah comes alive before their eyes, and God "speaks" again.

Young People Feel God

I once asked a group of teens who had become bar and bat mitzvah, "How did you feel the presence of God during your bar or bat mitzvah ceremony?"

- ✦ "I felt that God was around when I held the Torah and when I was reading it. The Torah scroll symbolizes a special closeness to God."

- ✦ "Reading from the Torah was like God giving Moses the

Torah. It's come down to us, and we're taking its laws into our hands. Because the Torah symbolizes God."

At such moments we understand the Torah blessing *Baruch attah Adonai, notein hatorah:* "Blessed are You, Adonai, Giver of the Torah." God did not give Torah once only, long ago. God gives Torah *today.* This is Torah's magical power that has spoken through the ages.

Torah lets us hear God speak, either with hushed comforting quiet or with a great cosmic roar that humbles us. This is how we hear God. This is how we stand at Sinai again. All that the Jewish people have been and all that we will be is on the *bimah* as you read from the scroll. The Torah has been battered and burned and torn through the ages. But it has survived because we have cherished it.

★

Where do you think that Torah came from?
Does it matter where it came from? _____

What are your favorite Torah stories? How can you feel God's Presence in those stories?

_____

We can feel God's Presence in stories that touch us emotionally and that teach us something about moral wisdom. What stories in the Torah touch you emotionally? How do they make you feel? What stories in the Torah offer moral wisdom? What do you learn from them?

_____

If you know what your bar or bat mitzvah Torah portion is, read it in English. Choose one verse that will be your "slogan" for the next year.

_____

If you know what your *haftarah* portion is, read it in English. Choose one verse that will be your "slogan" for the next year.

_____

5

Putting the *Mitzvah* Back in Bar and Bat Mitzvah

*God is hiding in the world. Our task
is to let the divine emerge from our deeds.*

—Abraham Joshua Heschel, *God In Search of Man*

The Difference between *Mitzvah* and *Mitzveh*

Ask your parents, siblings, friends—even your rabbi—this trick question: How do you pronounce the Hebrew word for "commandment"? Chances are you will get two different pronunciations: *mitzveh* and *mitzvah*. So, which is it: *mitzvah* or *mitzveh*?

One small vowel makes all the difference. *Mitzveh* is a Yiddish term that comes from the original Hebrew term *mitzvah*. As author Rabbi Moshe Waldoks once wrote, "*Mitzveh* means doing something for someone else; feeling communal solidarity by imitating God's concern for the world."

Mitzvah means something deeper. *Mitzvah*, "obligation," is essential to Jewish living. It is a religious commandment, a link between God and humanity, a sacred obligation. Traditionally, there are 613 *mitzvot*. All of them are derived from the Torah. There are ritual *mitzvot*, such as observing Shabbat and keeping the dietary laws of *kashrut*. Those *mitzvot* connect us to God. There are also ethical *mitzvot,* such as not murdering or gossiping. Those *mitzvot* connect us with people. Some *mitzvot* are in positive language: "Thou *shalt* . . ." Others are in negative language: "Thou shalt *not* . . ." Some *mitzvot* can be done today; some could be performed only during the days when the Temple in Jerusalem stood. Some *mitzvot* can be done anywhere; others can be done only in the Land of Israel.

You are becoming bar or bat mitzvah. Soon you will be old enough to do the *mitzvot.* The reason you do them dates back to Sinai, where God made a covenant with the people of Israel. A covenant, or *brit,* is a contract, a deal. God says: I will always make sure that there is a Jewish people, as long as you do the *mitzvot.* The idea of *mitzvah* is central to Jewish identity. It is the essence of Judaism.

A *mitzveh* is something nice that you want to do: "Why don't you do a *mitzveh* and call your great-uncle?" But as a Chicago rabbi once said, "Judaism is more than the Boy Scout Handbook." It is more than niceness. It is about *mitzvah.*

Sometimes what we thought was a *mitzveh* was really a *mitzvah.* My wife's grandmother would always take strangers from the streets into her home for Shabbat dinner. My mother-in-law thought that she was doing it because she was being nice; she was performing a *mitzveh.* But she was *really* doing a *mitzvah:* fulfilling the holy obligation to offer hospitality. At that moment, my wife's grandmother was linked to all Jewish history. It was as if she were the matriarch, Sarah, welcoming strangers into her tent in the ancient wilderness.

Why Perform *Mitzvot*?

Traditional Judaism says that there is really only one reason to perform *mitzvot:* God commanded us to do so. The *mitzvot* represent the will of God. To know what you have to do, you must study the Torah and the hundreds of years of writing of Jewish law that describe how the *mitzvot* should be done.

Conservative, Reconstructionist, and Reform Judaism have produced many other reasons for doing *mitzvot.* Among them:

✦ *Mitzvot* help us feel God's presence. When you light Shabbat candles, you feel inspired, as if the light from the candles is going right to your heart. *Havdalah,* the ceremony that ends Shabbat, can be truly uplifting, especially when you look at the braided candle that is used at *havdalah* and think about how it could symbolize that *all* Jews are braided together through our history, our relationships, our teachings. When you do a *mitzvah,* it's like inviting God into your life. Knowing that a *mitzvah* will bring God's Presence can encourage us to do it again and again.

✦ *Mitzvot* remind us of the covenant at Sinai. There, our people began a disciplined pattern of life. Every time we do a *mitzvah,* we remember that original covenant with God. We perform righteous deeds not only because our conscience tells us to do so. The conscience is often not enough. We do them because an external force makes us want to. That force (we could call it God) acts like a time machine and brings us back to Sinai.

✦ *Mitzvot* help us feel connected to *all* Jews—past, present, and future. One Jew recently explained to me that he refused to eat pork, even though he really liked it, because he had thought much about "the enemies of our people who tortured us by forcing us to eat pork. I feel a connection with those Jews. They are my people. To eat pork would be like disrespecting my ancestors and what they went through. That is why I stopped eating it."

✦ *Mitzvot* connect us to Jewish tradition. This tradition is several thousand years old and has produced some of the world's greatest values: justice, compassion, freedom, hope, community. The *practices* produced the values. Since we cherish those values, why throw away the practices that inspired them? Shabbat, for example, teaches us that time is holy. It can help restore the Jewish soul. *Kashrut,* or the dietary laws, can help us retain our identity as Jews and remind us that not everything in the world is permitted to us, that we simply can't gorge ourselves on everything we want. Kosher slaughtering teaches that we should avoid unnecessary cruelty to animals. Studying Torah can make us think deeper about what it means to be Jewish, and it can give us a true sense of our identity as Jews. Just think of all the *mitzvot* that teach us about human relations, such as correct behavior in business, that are increasingly relevant with every passing year. Before we ignore those *mitzvot,* we should think long and hard about them. Much is at stake here.

Mitzvah: The Torah's Active Voice

Mitzvot teach us to sanctify life. They teach us how to care for others, about God, and about ourselves.

A Jewish teaching says that 650,000 Jews were present at Sinai, and there are 650,000 letters in the Torah. That means that every Jew got his or her own letter in the Torah—which means that every Jew has a *mitzvah* with his or her name written on it.

Not every *mitzvah* will appeal to every Jew. But each one is sacred, because each one has a purpose. If you want to be a great soccer player, or ballet dancer, or actor, or pianist, or computer programmer, there is only one way to accomplish that. *Practice.*

And if we want to be holy, decent people, then the way to do that is to practice. We do it through the *mitzvot,* since *what we do shapes who we are.*

Doing *Mitzvot* Makes Jewish Values Real

There is no real "official" list of Jewish values. Decades ago, the Jewish writer Hayim Greenberg said that if you can name all the plants in Israel in Hebrew, then you could certainly be a great citizen of the State of Israel. But if you don't know the meaning of such Hebrew expressions as *mitzvah, tzedakah* (sacred giving or charity), and *chesed* (lovingkindness), then you cannot be a good Jew. "These are the powers that build a Jewish personality," he wrote.

The following list represents both ritual *mitzvot* and ethical *mitzvot*. It represents the Jewish tradition's best ways of building a Jewish personality and deepening human character.

Under each *mitzvah* are projects that give those *mitzvot* shape and meaning. At the end of this book are lists of groups and *tzedakot* (charities) that can help you fulfill many of these *mitzvot*. You can do some of those *mitzvot* by yourself; others will be more appropriate for your entire family to do together. Through them, you can connect Jewish wisdom to daily life.

 ### *Gemilut Chasadim:* Acts of Loving-Kindness

Gemilut chasadim is best understood as "nonfinancial giving." So powerful is *gemilut chasadim* that the Torah begins with it: God makes clothing for Adam and Eve. And the Torah ends with it: God buries Moses. So powerful is *gemilut chasadim* that performing acts of loving-kindness is the closest that humans can come to a genuine imitation of God.

✦ Visit someone who has lost a loved one. This fulfills the *mitzvah* of *nichum aveilim* (comforting mourners).

✦ Visit or call on someone who is ill. This fulfills the *mitzvah* of *bikur cholim* (visiting the sick).

✦ Arrange to have leftover food from your bar or bat mitzvah celebration taken to a soup kitchen that feeds the homeless and the hungry.

✦ Bring *chametz* (leavened food products that are forbidden during Pesach) from your home to a local food pantry. Encourage others in your synagogue to do this also.

✦ Volunteer at a soup kitchen for the homeless.

✦ Ask guests to bring canned food or such toiletries as soap, toothpaste, or shampoo to your bar or bat mitzvah party for subsequent distribution to the homeless.

✦ Time can be devoted to a certain cause or issue. Write to an elected official about an important social or political issue.

This fulfills the *mitzvah* of *redifat tzedek* (pursuing justice). Use a Jewish idea in the letter.

✦ Participate in a clothing drive for the needy.

Tzedakah: Sacred Giving

Some Jews say *tzedakah* is the highest *mitzvah*. It is best translated as "sacred giving." *Tzedakah* is not what we give; it is our responsibility as part of our covenant with God. Though many American Jews have dropped a variety of ritual practices, they cling to the practice of *tzedakah* as they would to a precious heirloom. Perhaps this is because, as Proverbs says, *"Tzedakah redeems from death."* It not only potentially saves individuals from a physical death, but also redeems the giver from a death of the soul. Selfishness causes people to "shrivel up" inside. It makes them mean and sour. Giving to others keeps our own humanity alive.

✦ Choose a recipient for *tzedakah* from the list at the end of this book. Contribute to it in honor of becoming bar or bat mitzvah, or set aside for *tzedakah* a portion of money you receive as gifts at your bar or bat mitzvah. Some young people have even given away all their gift money. Several years ago, twins in California used all their gift money to help the "boat people," Cambodians who were fleeing a brutal government in their country.

✦ Give three percent of the cost of your bar or bat mitzvah celebration to MAZON, a Jewish Response to Hunger, which distributes the money to food banks and hunger relief organizations all over the world.

✦ Contribute some *tzedakah* every Friday night before Shabbat into a family *puschke,* or a *tzedakah* container. Decide as a family where the money should go.

Talmud Torah: The Study of Torah

Jewish learning should extend beyond the words of Hebrew texts. Jewish wisdom can walk through all kinds of doors in our lives.

★ Research the origins of the Jewish community in which you live, or the start of your own congregation.

★ Read some Jewish books that are not part of your regular religious school curriculum. Some suggestions:

Lawrence Kushner, *The Book of Miracles* (Jewish Lights Publishing). A wonderful book about Jewish spirituality for young readers. It teaches very difficult ideas in a gentle and funny way.

Carolyn Meyer, *Drummers of Jericho* (Gulliver Books/Harcourt). A novel about Jewish identity and anti-Semitism in a Southern town. A young Jewish woman fights for her religious rights when her school marching band's songs are limited to only Christian hymns.

Chaim Potok, *The Chosen* (Fawcett Book Group). A novel about the relationship between two Jewish boys—one Hasidic, one modern Orthodox. It takes place in Brooklyn in the 1940s, under the shadow of the Holocaust and during the birth of the State of Israel. A classic story of friendship.

Art Spiegelman, *Maus I* and *Maus II* (Pantheon Books). Spiegelman tells the story of the Holocaust in comic book form. The Jews are portrayed as mice and the Nazis as cats. It is powerful and gripping.

Sydney Taylor, *All-of-a-Kind Family* (Dell Books). A book about five Jewish sisters growing up in New York City in 1912.

Marcus Zusak, *The Book Thief* (Knopf Books). One of the best Holocaust novels for young adults in recent years. The story of a network of good friends in Nazi Germany.

★ Creating your own *tallit* is also an act of Torah. A girl in Tennessee actually wove her bat mitzvah *tallit* from cotton that was grown on her family's ancestral plantation in the deep South!

★ Visit a Jewish historical site or Jewish museum, or visit Holocaust museums/memorials.

✹ Do research on the internet on Jewish history, Israel, or the Holocaust. So much is available on the internet these days. Some interesting sites for kids to visit include:

http://www.annefrank.com—a site about Anne Frank.
http://www.jvibe.com—a great site for Jewish teenagers, filled with news and cultural stuff.
http://www.babaganewz.com—probably one of the best sites for Jewish kids. It contains material on Jewish holidays and various other themes.
http://www.my-bar-mitzvah.com—a resource guide for bar/bat mitzvah.
http://www.jewishhigh.com—a blog for Jewish kids to hang out online together.
http://www.holysparks.com/kidlinks.html—a great source for Jewish spirituality for kids. It even has homework help on it!

 ### *Hidur Penei Zakein:* Honoring the Elderly

The elderly deserve respect regardless of their accomplishments or status. They are often part of our own families. Their stories and their lives are closely interwoven with our own.

✹ Call, write, or visit an elderly relative or friend.

✹ Help nursing home residents hold services for Shabbat and Jewish holidays and Passover seders.

✹ Deliver flowers to nursing home residents before the start of Shabbat.

✹ "Adopt" and visit a resident of a nearby nursing home.

✹ Donate old books, records, audiotapes, CDs, books on tape, or videotapes to a nursing home.

 ### *Zicharon:* Memory

So precious is the *mitzvah* of memory that Torah commands us no less than 169 times to remember. Perhaps there is significance in 13 being the square root of 169. At the age of thirteen, you can observe and remember Shabbat and the major Jewish holidays. At Passover, and, in fact, all year round, you can especially remember that we were slaves in Egypt.

✦ What is your Hebrew name? For whom were you named? What special Jewish qualities did that person have?

✦ Find out your family's name in the "old country." Do not let it fade into oblivion.

✦ Find out the name of the town, city, or village your family came from in its country of origin. Someone in your family may know this, and it is more than simply "some place in Russia." Look up the town in the *Encyclopedia Judaica* and learn something about the town and what it gave to the Jewish world. The *Encyclopedia Judaica* is also on CD-ROM, and there is genealogy software that might also be helpful as well.

✦ Many Jews are now immigrating to this country. Many are from the former Soviet Union and Argentina. Collect clothing, food, furniture, books, and such Jewish items as menorahs for needy immigrants.

✦ Share your bar or bat mitzvah symbolically with a righteous Christian who saved Jewish lives during the Holocaust, which is also known as the *Shoah*. (See the list of *tzedakot* for the address of the Jewish Fund for the Righteous.)

Shabbat: Honoring the Sabbath

The Zionist thinker Achad Ha-Am once wrote, "More than Israel has kept the Sabbath, so has the Sabbath kept Israel." Every Jewish life should have more than a small taste of Shabbat.

✦ Have Shabbat dinners in your home, preferably every Friday night. Light the Shabbat candles, and recite the *kiddush* (the blessing over wine) and *motzi* (the blessing over bread). Learn and sing *birchat ha-mazon*, the blessing after the meal. Invite friends to share in your Shabbat celebration.

✦ Learn to cook a traditional Shabbat dish, such as noodle kugel, *challah*, or *matzah* ball soup.

✦ Create *mitzvot* for Shabbat. Decide what you should do or should not do. Examples:

- Try to avoid shopping for items that are not essential on Shabbat, like entertainment items, videotapes, CDs, and other amusements. (Can you stay away from the mall? Even harder, perhaps: on Shabbat, can you refrain from ordering things online?)

- Experiment with making Shabbat a computer-less (or video game-less) day.

- If you can't live without your computer, how about not playing violent games on it?

- Experiment with making Shabbat a "no television" day.

- Concentrate on being with friends or family instead.

- Attend synagogue services as a family.

- Reserve a half-hour on Saturday to think about something Jewish. Examples: read a Jewish story; read the newspaper and think of the Jewish issues that might be associated with various news stories; think about a Jewish value and how you might try to make it real during the coming week.

- End Shabbat with *havdalah* (the early Saturday evening service that marks the end of Shabbat). *Havdalah* is a beautiful, brief, home-based service that uses candles, wine, and spices. It is a wonderful way to say farewell to Shabbat.

Kol Yisrael Arevim: All Jews Are Responsible for Each Other

The ties that bind us to Jews in other lands are sacred ties. They remind us that no matter where we may be living, we are all one people with one destiny.

Few things bind the Jewish people together more than our historic love of the Land of Israel. Bar and bat mitzvah can mark the time when we deepen our learning about the meaning of Zionism and strengthen our connections to the Land of Israel.

✦ Deepen your relationship with Jews in other lands. What foreign language are you learning in school? Write letters to the bar/bat mitzvah–age classes in a congregation in a country where that language is used. Your rabbi can help make this happen by contacting the synagogue movement of which you are a member (Reform, Conservative, Reconstructionist, or Orthodox) and finding out where there are synagogues with young people who might become pen pals.

✦ Purchase and use Israeli products, such as Israeli oranges, candies, clothing, and computer software.

✦ Plant trees in Israel through the Jewish National Fund.

✦ Give *tzedakah* to the needy in Israel.

✦ Learn about and help support a congregation like yours in Israel. Donate money to its religious school so that it can purchase supplies. Your national synagogue movement can help you do this.

✦ Travel to Israel as a family.

✦ Speak out for Israel! Write letters to your local or school newspaper about Israel and the plight of world Jewry. When you read newspaper articles or watch or hear news programs that are biased against Israel, speak out! Write letters! Let your voice be heard!

Kedushat Halashon: The Holiness of Speech

Most people assume that "holy speech" means prayer. But it goes way beyond that. Joseph Telushkin, the author of many popular books on Judaism, suggests that if you can't go twenty-four hours without saying something unkind about someone else, then you have a real problem. Many people have such a problem; the Torah's most violated commandment is Leviticus 19:16: "Do not go about as a talebearer among your people."

We should watch our mouths just as we watch our hands. We should learn to avoid gossip, talebearing, rumormongering, and other acts of verbal violence. In Hebrew, we call such prohibited speech *lashon hara* ("the evil tongue").

✦ Learn to be careful about what you say about other people.

✦ Discuss with your family whether certain kinds of speech are acceptable. Discuss the quality and content (and the volume!) of speech in your home. Consider how speech can be used for healing, not hurting.

Kedushat Hazeman: The Holiness of Festivals and Sacred Seasons

To be a Jew is to feel a part of Judaism's entire festival calendar. To be a Jew is to go through the cycle of the seasons as a Jew.

✦ Participate in a Passover seder with your family. Write a special reading to be used at the seder.

✦ Write a prayer to use when your family lights its Chanukah menorah.

✦ Build a *sukkah* in your backyard. Decorate it. Have dinner in it, or at least make *motzi* and *kiddush* (the blessings over bread and wine) in it. If the weather is warm, sleep in it overnight in order to fulfill the Biblical *mitzvah* of "dwelling in the *sukkah.*"

✦ Attend Purim services dressed as a character from the Megillah.

✦ Plant a tree in Israel each year on Tu B'Shevat, the New Year of trees.

Tzar Baalei Chayim: Noncruelty to Animals

Judaism teaches us to treat animals with dignity. They cannot be wantonly destroyed through hunting; animals of unequal strength cannot be yoked together; an animal that has collapsed under the burden of a load must be helped even if it belongs to an enemy. Judaism even addresses the psychological pain of animals and advises that a mother bird must be sent away to spare her the pain of seeing the eggs being removed from her nest so a human can eat them. Kosher slaughtering ensures swift, painless deaths for animals.

* ✶ Become involved with an organization that deals with animal rights.

* ✶ Become conscious of the type of clothing that you wear. Debate the *kashrut* of fur and leather clothing. Is it "kosher" to wear clothing from animals that have been brutally killed?

* ✶ Experiment with keeping kosher. Record your experiences and impressions.

* ✶ Give money to your local animal shelter.

Tikkun Atzmi: Repairing the Self

An important part of becoming bar and bat mitzvah is growing as an individual. Ancient rabbis believed that the ultimate goal of the *mitzvot* was nothing less than *letzaref haberiot*, turning someone into a better person.

* ✶ Eliminate a bad habit.

* ✶ Patch up a bad relationship by establishing *shalom*, peace with another person. Discuss what happened in your relationship and the steps that you will both take in order to make it better.

* ✶ Transform a negative attitude into a positive attitude. For example, perhaps you resist cleaning up your room. Instead of saying, "This is stupid, useless work," learn to view it as a way of keeping order in your life. Perhaps you have a not-so-good attitude toward school work. Change your attitude so that you can view your school success as helpful to your future.

Mitzvah: The Path to Self-Esteem

There is another reason for doing *mitzvot* that most people never even consider. Doing *mitzvot* helps us feel better about ourselves.

Some kids with certain learning disabilities can't learn Hebrew, and that makes it difficult for them to prepare for bar and bat mitzvah. But many children who are learning-disabled do learn Hebrew. When I work with such children, I give them as much as they can do, even if it means less Torah to read or fewer prayers to lead at the ceremony. I do this because I believe that bar and bat mitzvah is *what you are* and *how you prepare to be a responsible Jew*. It really does *not* depend on how much Hebrew you can learn.

But what if a child simply *can't* learn Hebrew? This problem is not so new. How did our ancestors deal with this issue?

In the past, a child in a traditional Jewish society who could not learn Hebrew had a job to do: He would go from house to house and collect wax for the candles that would burn in the synagogue. Without candles, the synagogue would plunge into darkness, physically as well as spiritually. When the synagogue candles were lit, the worshipers would remember the saying *Torah or*, "Torah is light." The child might not be able to read Torah, but he could help the community feel the light of Torah.

What can we learn from this? *Children owed something to the Jewish community*. We might now call this "good citizenship."

How do we translate that lesson to our time? If we use our ancestors' practices as a model, then we would involve a seriously learning-disabled child in *mitzvot* in the community. At the bar and bat mitzvah ceremony, the youngster could speak about the *mitzvot* performed during the preparation for truly becoming bar or bat mitzvah, for being old enough to understand the meaning of *mitzvah*.

The Path to Maturity and Community

The word *mitzvah* comes from the root *tzavah*. There are two translations of that root. It means "to command" and also "to connect." *Mitzvot*, then, are the ways that we connect with God, with the better parts of ourselves, and with other people.

I learned much about the meaning of *mitzvot* when a close relative of my great-uncle Harry died. One evening during the *shiva* (the seven-day mourning) period, among those sitting *shiva* was a young boy in his early teens. He went over to my great-uncle Harry and said to him, "May God comfort you on your loss." He then distributed prayer books to the mourners in the living room and began to lead the evening service.

After the service was over, he went into the dining room, helped himself to some cookies, returned to my great-uncle's side, shook the old man's hand, and left. I turned to my great-uncle and asked, "Who was that boy?" Uncle Harry shrugged his shoulders and answered, "A kid from the *shul* [synagogue]."

What did I learn from my Uncle Harry's shrug and from his response? The *shrug* meant that Uncle Harry did not think that the boy's name was particularly important. The most important thing about him was that he was "a kid from the *shul*." *That* was how he knew the boy. That was how he identified him.

Suddenly, it all made sense. The boy was about thirteen or fourteen. He was, therefore, bar mitzvah—old enough to do *mitzvot*. He must have learned the following lesson: "Now that you are bar mitzvah, and old enough to do *mitzvot*, you are going to learn the most delicate *mitzvah* imaginable. You're going to learn how to go into a house of mourning and use your prayer-leading skills to walk people through the 'valley of the shadow of death' (as it says in Psalm 23). A lot of Jewish kids can lead a service. But this skill will help heal people, and in that you can help heal the world."

I have often thought about what that boy learned about Jewish community. For that is yet another purpose of *mitzvot:* bonding us with the community.

That is what it means to become bar or bat mitzvah.

✦

In your opinion, why should we Jews do *mitzvot*?

_____

Which *mitzvot* will you choose to do? _____

When have you felt connected to the Jewish community or Jewish people?

_____

_____

What does it mean to you when you say "I am Jewish"?

_____

_____

Use the space that follows to start a *mitzvah* journal to help you plan what you will do and record your experiences. Attach more pages if you need them.

My *Mitzvah* Journal

_____

_____

_____

_____

_____

_____

_____

_____

_____

_____

My *Mitzvah* Journal

_____

_____

_____

_____

_____

_____

_____

_____

_____

_____

_____

_____

_____

_____

_____

_____

_____

_____

_____

_____

_____

_____

_____

_____

_____

My *Mitzvah* Journal

_____

_____

_____

_____

_____

_____

_____

_____

_____

_____

_____

_____

_____

_____

_____

_____

_____

_____

_____

_____

_____

_____

_____

_____

_____

6

Rites and Wrongs of Passage

PUTTING THE PARTY IN PERSPECTIVE

"It doesn't matter what happens at the temple;
it's the party that counts."

—from the movie *Keeping up with the Steins*

I didn't think that I was going to like it, but, I admit it, I found the movie *Keeping up with the Steins* very amusing—even heartwarming. It's the story of a Los Angeles Jewish family that is preparing for its son's bar mitzvah. The family members are convinced that their party has to be bigger, fancier, and more entertaining than that of their "rivals," the Steins. But it turns out that the bar mitzvah boy doesn't want that at all. Encouraged by his somewhat unusual grandfather, he wants to know the deeper reason behind bar mitzvah.

Sadly, no one in the boy's family realizes that curiosity. They're all too busy coming up with a party even bigger (they hope) than the Steins'.

Are we talking about a religious ceremony here, or what?

How did this happen?

Every Jew in America has a "can you top this?" tale about the Worst Bar Mitzvah Party of the Year. I won't even list the contenders here. Some are so ridiculous that they are almost funny.

But before we start criticizing bar and bat mitzvah parties too much, we should know something. *The party is an important part of bar and bat mitzvah.* It was not just suddenly invented by a caterer in 1952.

The first mention of the bar mitzvah party in any Jewish text is in the *Shulchan Aruch* (the classic sixteenth-century code of Jewish law): "It is the religious obligation of the father to make a festive meal in honor of his son's becoming bar mitzvah, just as he might do when the boy marries."

Some say the tradition of the bar mitzvah party goes back to Rabbi Yosef in the Talmud (*Kiddushin* 31a). Rabbi Yosef was blind. Jewish law said that the blind were exempt from doing *mitzvot*. But Rabbi Yosef realized that he was already doing the *mitzvot*. Why not get "credit" for doing so? He wanted to change his status from someone who didn't have to do the *mitzvot* to someone who *had* to do the *mitzvot*.

So Rabbi Yosef made an offer. If someone could prove that a blind person had an obligation to do *mitzvot*, then he would host a great celebration to mark his change in status.

A little more than 1,000 years later, a sixteenth-century legal authority on Jewish law, Rabbi Solomon Luria, thought about this discussion in the Talmud. This is what he figured out: If Rabbi Yosef could celebrate that *he* was now obligated to do the *mitzvot*, then we should celebrate and give thanks to God that a bar mitzvah is now obligated to fulfill the *mitzvot*. Rabbi Luria ruled that the bar mitzvah meal is a *seudat mitzvah* (a religiously commanded festive meal) that has the same spiritual importance as a wedding feast. The boy would have to give a Torah speech (*derasha*) during the banquet. This was probably the origin of the bar and bat mitzvah speech.

The bar mitzvah feast occurred in the afternoon as the third meal of the Sabbath. An hour before the afternoon service (*minchah*), the boy would go to the homes of his guests to personally invite them to the third meal. At the meal, the lad would give a mini-lecture on the customs of bar mitzvah and would lead the blessing after the meal (*birchat ha-mazon*).

A Choice: Celebration or "Blow-out"

Everyone talks about how overdone bar and mitzvah parties have become. But we Jews have been thinking and worrying about this for hundreds of years.

Even in medieval times, there were excesses in celebration. In the sixteenth century, Solomon Luria didn't like what he saw. In his commentary on the Talmud, he condemned bar mitzvah parties as "occasions for wild levity, just for the purpose of stuffing the gullet."

The rabbis of the Middle Ages eventually made laws to limit spending on festivities, as well as on styles of dress and even the kind of jewelry Jews were allowed to wear. In the 1440s, one Italian Jewish community limited the number of wedding guests to twenty men, ten women, five girls, and all the relatives up to second cousins. They also permitted the wearing of fur-lined jackets, in any color other than black, and only if they didn't have any silk fringes.

Why did these laws come into existence? The rabbis believed that people should dress and act according to their standing in the community and not try to live beyond their means. (Compare this to what is sadly true nowadays: Some people actually go through major financial problems after a particularly elaborate bar or bat mitzvah extravaganza).

The community also wanted to protect the dignity of the less wealthy. This is similar to the reason in Judaism for a plain wooden casket at a funeral: so no one would be embarrassed by having a less-than-fancy coffin. That same concern for the dignity of the less wealthy expressed itself at weddings. Nowadays everyone has a wedding ring. Not so in the old days. *Communities* would own beautiful, specially decorated wedding rings, which would be briefly placed upon the finger of each new bride in the community. Why? So poor families would not be humiliated.

In the early decades of the twentieth century, when our ancestors were first becoming successful in America, bar mitzvah parties became especially fancy. Soon, the bar mitzvah party became even more important than the ceremony itself. Caterers realized that bar mitzvah was big business. Then people began to give gifts—sometimes lavish. Many Jewish men remember that they got fountain pens as bar mitzvah gifts. In earlier days, it was a sign of "manhood," probably because the fountain pen was so widely used in the business world and could be used for signing contracts. And the rest—as they say—is history.

The Ethics of Jewish Celebration

Yes, bar and bat mitzvah has become a multi-million dollar industry: catering halls, musicians, dancers, photographers and videographers, caricaturists, dancers, comedians, party planners, personalized *kippot*, party favors, florists.

Everyone wants his or her party to be unique. But don't worry—you already *are* unique, because you are made in God's Image. Your sacred uniqueness doesn't require a fancy bar or bat mitzvah party to prove it.

But there is a larger issue in the way that Jews celebrate. It helps us understand the way our people look at the world.

Judaism believes in *moderation*.

Consider the subject of *food*. According to Jewish law and tradition, we should neither starve ourselves nor gorge ourselves. Instead, we should eat in a holy way—through moderation and perhaps even through keeping kosher, which teaches us that not all foods and ways of eating are acceptable.

Consider *alcohol*. Judaism says that we should not totally reject alcohol. But we also shouldn't drink to get drunk (except for adults getting a little drunk on Purim.) We should drink in *moderation*. We should try to make the way we drink into something holy—through *kiddush*, and wine at Pesach, and the joyful *L'chayim!*

Consider *money and materialism*. Judaism says that we shouldn't reject possessions and live with nothing. But we shouldn't buy everything we see, either. We should own in *moderation*. We can make our money holy through *tzedakah* (holy giving).

Too many modern Jews refuse to listen to that message. This is what they say: "Judaism is for the synagogue—for religious school and for services. When I go outside the sanctuary, then I don't have to listen to religion. I can be a 'regular person.' And if I want to boogie down with the big bucks, that's my business."

This is sad. I sometimes wonder: Imagine someone who is considering converting to Judaism, as thousands of people do every year. Imagine that person attending a loud and expensive bar or bat mitzvah party that goes on until three in the morning. I wonder: Would that person regard our faith as a worthwhile, spiritual religion?

I don't usually attend such affairs. But when I do, I usually say to myself, "What happened to bar and bat mitzvah being a sacred Jewish life passage?"

Toward the Middle Way: How to Make Our Celebrations Holy

What do we do? Is there a Jewish way of "party planning"? Yes, there is.

Sit down with your parents and ask them this question: "What Jewish values do we hope this bar or bat mitzvah celebration will contain and reveal?" Make a list of them. Your list might include compassion, dignity, justice, learning, social action, generosity, humility, moderation, a love for the Jewish people and the Jewish homeland. Plan your celebration around these values, and stick to these plans.

Let's talk about *menu*.

Remember, Judaism believes in sanctifying the act of drinking and eating. Those acts can be holy. They become holy when we say *kiddush* and *motzi* and sing *birchat ha-mazon*, the blessing after the meal. Blessing our food is how we remember that we are linked to a Divine Presence that sustains us.

But now, let's go one step further. Consider *kashrut*—the Jewish dietary laws that instruct us not to eat such biblically prohibited foods as pork or shellfish, not to mix milk and meat products, and to eat only meat that has been slaughtered according to Jewish law.

For Conservative and Orthodox Judaism, *kashrut* is a basic part of living Jewishly. Both movements officially expect that bar and bat mitzvah parties—indeed, *any* celebration—will be kosher.

Reconstructionist Judaism maintains *kashrut* as an important value that connects individual Jews to the entire Jewish people and to the Jewish past. Reconstructionism believes that there is an important connection between how we eat and how we live. Reconstructionists would want *all* Jews to feel comfortable eating at any celebration. Therefore, Reconstructionist synagogues require that food served in the synagogue be kosher.

While Reform Judaism does not demand that *kashrut* be observed, it is increasingly open to the spiritual benefits of the Jewish dietary laws. For Reform Judaism, *kashrut* is a *mitzvah* that each individual Jew can choose to do. Many Reform synagogues observe "biblical *kashrut*," forbidding those foods that are prohibited by the Bible, such as pork products and shellfish.

By having a *kosher* bar or bat mitzvah celebration, you would be saying: God cares about what we eat.

Judaism is for all of life, not only what we do in the synagogue.

Eating is not just an animal act. It is not merely "pigging out." It is a holy act. We can sanctify *what* and *how* we eat.

All Jews should be able to eat at our celebrations. We are one people who should have one cuisine.

What about *music*? What kind of music is appropriate at a bar or bat mitzvah celebration? Is there "kosher" Jewish party music? Should rap or hip-hop music be played at bar and bat mitzvah parties?

Should bar or bat mitzvah guests have to listen to violent lyrics? What about the volume of the music? Should guests have to shout while trying to talk with whomever is sitting next to them? Is laryngitis an appropriate bar or bat mitzvah party favor?

Should there be Israeli and Jewish folk music? What about dancing the traditional Jewish dance, the *hora*?

What about *dress*? Is there a "kosher" way of dressing?

Should kids be pushed into adulthood by wearing tuxedos or overly adult dresses? (I always tell mothers and daughters: Please, no plunging neck lines or short skirts on the *bimah*, the platform from which the service is conducted. Call me a prude if you want, but there is a time and a place for everything.)

What about *themes*? It may be hard to believe, I know, but Jews celebrated becoming bar mitzvah for centuries before the first caterer ever thought of themes! Are such themes as casinos, shopping, sports teams, or movies appropriate? Are there better themes? How about "Caring in Our Community"? Could you put information about various *tzedakot* (charities) and social service agencies on the tables, along with self-addressed, stamped envelopes, and invite people to donate in your honor to those *tzedakot*?

What about *decorations*? One family put the emblems of the twelve tribes of Israel on the luncheon tables at their son's bar mitzvah party. It was their way of teaching about our ancient roots in the Land of Israel. I know a family that bought trees in Israel in honor of each bar mitzvah guest, and put certificates verifying the tree's purchase at each person's table setting. One bat mitzvah girl I know put pictures of endangered animals at each table, and urged guests to contribute to environmental causes in her honor.

What about the *candle lighting ceremony*? There is no reference to this ceremony in the Talmud—or anywhere else in Jewish literature, for that matter. It was probably invented by a caterer in the early 1950s. We don't know who it was.

But if you decide to have a candle-lighting ceremony, here is an idea: As each guest lights a candle, he or she might offer you a blessing, or a word of encouragement, or a Jewish value that you might embody.

What about *guests*? Is there a Jewish way of inviting guests to your bar or bat mitzvah celebration? No one can ever like everyone, but are you making sure that you do not hurt people by not inviting them? It seems to me that bar and bat mitzvah should not be used for hurting someone socially.

What about *location*? Where should the party be? It is often held in a catering hall or a restaurant, but there is a special sanctity about having it in the synagogue itself. What about having it at home or at a summer camp? The Jewish home has a special holiness to it, and a camp provides the opportunity to get back to nature and make the whole celebration more informal and relaxed.

Best yet, many families travel to Israel instead of having a party. You may forget parties, but never a trip to Israel. In some communities, parents of bar and bat mitzvah candidates make an agreement with each other about how they will celebrate this rite of passage. Since the young people are all in the same class, and will therefore see how the others are celebrating their bar or bat mitzvah, they want to ensure that there is a set of standards. So they agree: "No themes. No parties until the wee hours. No outrageous music or spending."

Some parents have even created a party co-op in which they help create bar and bat mitzvah celebrations for each other—planning menus, cooking, transporting children, providing hospitality for out-of-town guests, even ushering at each other's bar and bat mitzvah ceremonies.

All of these are wonderful ways to build community. Community is more than feeling good. It is more than friendship. It is about sharing values.

Ultimately, the educational and religious spirit of bar and bat mitzvah can extend beyond the final hymn or prayer at the service. It can really make a difference in your life.

A friend told me that when a caterer asked him, "What's the theme of your daughter's bat mitzvah going to be?" he responded, "How about Judaism?"

It's a good answer: simple yet elegant.

✶

What are some of the values that you want your celebration to reflect?

_____

_____

_____

_____

How could you make that happen at your celebration?

_____

_____

_____

_____

What are some of the best parties you have been to?

_____

_____

_____

_____

The worst? _____

_____

_____

_____

What makes them good or bad? _____

_____

_____

_____

7

To a Skeptical Jewish Kid

He drew a circle that shut me out
Heretic, rebel, a thing to flout.
But love and I had the wit to win
We drew a circle that drew him in.

—Edwin Markham, "Outwitted"

In Donald Margulies' play *The Loman Family Picnic,* a boy named Stewie is about to become bar mitzvah. But Stewie is angry. He does not like his teacher, and he is frustrated because much of what he is learning seems to be meaningless.

Stewie: "Tell me what I'm reading," I said, "Tell me what the words mean." He looks at me like I'm not speaking any known language. "What does it mean?!," I said, "what am I saying?!" "What does it matter?" he says, "you can read it." "Yeah, but what does it mean?!" "It means you will be bar mitzvah!," he says. "But the words don't mean anything to me, they're just these funny little sounds." "Those funny sounds," he says, "are what make a boy different from a Jew!" "So?! You taught me how to read but you didn't teach me how to understand! What kind of Jew is that?!" This does not go over big. His lips are turning blue. I think he's gonna have an angina attack. All he cares about is rolling out bar mitzvah boys to repopulate the earth. We look the part and we can sing, but we don't know what we're saying! I have had it!

Doris (his mother): You have to go through with your bar mitzvah, Stewie. . . . You know how hard I've been working to make you a beautiful party?!

Stewie: Me? It's not for me. Make your beautiful party! I just won't be there. Tell everybody I got the runs!

Doris: Don't do this to me, Stewie! Don't make me cancel! We'll lose all our deposits! Is that what you want?! Hm?! Your father's blood money down the drain?! The hall, the band, the flowers?! The caterers?! I already bought my dress, what do you want me to do with it? Hock it? I've spent days laying out response cards like solitaire and clipping tables together! This is no time to be a prima donna, Stewie. One more week. That's all I ask. Give me the *nachas* [Yiddish word for "pleasure"] then you can do whatever . . . you want. You want to renounce Judaism? Renounce Judaism. Become a monk, I don't care.

Stewie: Remember, Ma, I'm doing this for you. I'll go through with it, and sing nice, and make you proud, and make the relatives cry, but once I'm bar mitzvahed, that's it, Ma, I'm never stepping foot in that place. Never again.

Doris: Thank you, darling, thank you.

It's not only in *Keeping up with the Steins.* I've probably seen every movie in which bar or bat mitzvah makes a "guest appearance." Here's what I have noticed: in almost every movie about bar mitzvah kids, the thirteen-year-old runs away and refuses to go through with the ceremony. So, Stewie is not alone. He is not only angry at his bar mitzvah preparation process—he is having a good old-fashioned crisis of faith.

As we get older we often start wondering about the meaning of Judaism and Jewish wisdom in our lives. Some kids are like Stewie. They remember their Jewish education with anger or boredom, or a combination of both. Some pretend to be atheists, saying that they don't believe in God. Actually, all they really do is *escape.*

The Jew who sincerely struggles with the life of faith and the life of Torah is in good company. Our history is the history of people who have always struggled with the meaning of God and the meaning of Judaism itself.

It goes all the way back to the beginnings of our history. When God wanted to destroy Sodom and Gomorrah for their sinfulness, Abraham challenged God to do justice for the innocent people in those cities. When the Israelites built the Golden Calf, God wanted to destroy the Jewish people, but Moses demanded that God spare the Jewish people. When God tested Job by causing him to lose all that was precious to him—his children, his home, even his health—Job demanded justice from God as well.

Elisha ben Avuya, a rebellious sage in the second century C.E., lost his faith in God when he saw a child die. The child had fallen out of a tree as he was shooing the mother bird away from the nest before taking the bird's eggs. Sending away the mother bird from the nest when taking its eggs is a *mitzvah*—and it is one of only two *mitzvot* in the Torah that promises long life to those who fulfill it. Yet, God had sent that child to his death. What was the justice of that death?

In the wonderful musical *Fiddler on the Roof*, Tevye the Dairyman, tired of persecutions by Russian soldiers, says to God, "I know that we're the chosen people. But could You please choose some other people for a change?" The Holocaust survivor and wise, compassionate writer Elie Wiesel has taught that it is the human obligation to question God in the face of unimaginable suffering.

And let us not forget Jacob. On the banks of the Jabbok River, Jacob wrestled with a divine being. He walked away from the encounter wounded, transformed, and with a new name: Yisrael. That's us. *We* are Yisrael. *We* are the children of Israel—the children of Jacob, who was the God Wrestler.

Think about that image of wrestling. In true wrestling there is a great deal of closeness between the fighters. Judaism is similar to this. No other religion in the world encourages its people to constantly question both God and the meaning of that religion itself, to be uncomfortable in their easily gained opinions about faith, to live the life of faith with a nagging feeling that there is more to the world than we once thought.

That's what it means to be a God Wrestler.

Maybe you, too, are a God Wrestler.

People often ask me, "Why do religions have to divide people? Why can't we have one universal religion?" This sounds like a good idea, doesn't it? Combine all the religious practices in the world, and see what comes out.

But here is my question: What would a universal religion exclude? What pearls of wisdom that are particular to a certain tradition would be overlooked or rejected? And how do I know that all the good stuff that I love about Judaism would make it through the mix?

Not only that. Think of the potential problems such a religion would have. The central thing in Judaism is studying, learning, and living Torah. The central thing in Christianity is living life according to the way Jesus lived and taught. Those are two very different beliefs and ways of life.

These days, "one-size-fits-all" socks are made. But religion is not a pair of socks. You may think that you want a basic, no-frills religion, but basic religions are sort of like basic, no-brand ice cream—they have no flavor. A simple, basic, "one-size-fits-all" religion is impossible because there is no such thing as a simple, basic, "one-size-fits-all" human being. There won't be such a thing until the Messianic Age merges us into a great rainbow of humanity. But until that day happens, we all view life in different ways, depending on how we were raised through our different religions.

F. Forrester Church, a Unitarian minister, has put it this way:

> We all stand in the cathedral of the world. In the cathedral are a multitude of stained glass windows. We are born in one part of the cathedral, and our parents and teachers teach us how to see the light that shines through our window, the window that carries the story of our people. The same light shines through all the windows of the cathedral, but we interpret its story in many different ways. The light is the presence of God. And the ways we see its colors are the ways of our tribe.
>
> There are different responses to life in the cathedral of the world. Relativists [people who think that there is no such thing as absolute truth, and that any opinion about living is as good as any other

opinion] say, "All the windows are basically the same, so it doesn't matter where you stand." They may even wander from window to window. Fundamentalists [people who believe that God really spoke every word of the Bible] say, "The light shines only through my window." And fanatics break all the windows except theirs.

Our view of truth is influenced by the way our people view the world. The light that comes through our Jewish window is the light of Torah and of *mitzvot*. It is not the whole light. But it is our way of viewing the light, and that is why it is holy.

"Don't Religions Simply Create Evil?"

I once heard a bar mitzvah boy trip over one of the readings in *Gates of Prayer*, a Reform prayer book. He said, "In a world torn by violence and *prayer*." But the reading is written, "In a world torn by violence and *pain*." History has often taught us that prayer can tear the world apart and that people have killed and have died for their own particular gods.

But wait. Let's do a body count. On the one side: the victims of religion through the ages. Tally them up in a grisly list: the unnamed victims of the Crusades, the Inquisitions, pogroms, religious wars that we learn about in school.

And then, tally up the list of those who have died not because of religion, but because of economic forces, or wanting certain territories, or the desires of rulers. The historical record is clear: More people have died at the hands of the great anti-religious nations—Nazi Germany and Soviet Russia—than at the hands of all the religious leaders of history combined.

In fact, if we are to look at the pain of the world that religion has caused, then we have to be fair and also look at the strength and the love that religion has caused. That strength, love, goodness, and holiness is much stronger than any of the evil done by people who say they are religious. (By the same token, there are rich people who do terrible things, but we don't reject money; sports figures who kill, but we still play sports; rock stars who take drugs, but we still listen to their music.) We should always judge something by the *best* that is within it, not by the worst.

In 1978, Nomi Fein was about to become bat mitzvah in Boston. Her *haftarah* portion contained the famous reference to "the wolf lying down with the lamb"—an image of the Messianic Age. Nomi had just seen the television miniseries *Holocaust*, and she was feeling pretty pessimistic about the possibility of a Messianic Age.

And then, two Holocaust survivors spoke at her school. She was moved by their message—so moved that she wrote them a letter.

> While listening to your speeches, the thing that amazed me most was your continuing faith in God. And it occurred to me that if people such as you, who have lived through such terrible conditions as you have, still have the faith and love to believe not only in God, but in the goodness of people also, then people such as I, who have never had much reason to complain and be bitter, have much more reason to be grateful and have total faith in life.

There is a lot that we can be cynical about in the world. So why not learn about the sources of hope from the people who first brought the idea of hope into the world?

Simon Wiesenthal, the late, heroic Nazi hunter, spent the last sixty years tracking down and catching Nazi war criminals. He was not a religious Jew. He said that he lost his faith in the concentration camp known as Dachau. There, he once saw a man make people pay him bread to use the *siddur* (a prayer book) that he had smuggled into the camp. "If that's religion," Wiesenthal said to himself at the time, "I don't want to be religious."

Upon later hearing that story, someone asked Wiesenthal, "You may be right. It is horrible, unthinkable, for someone to charge another person bread to use a prayer book. But what about the people who freely gave their bread away? What does it say about them?"

What it says about them is that people need faith. You can live in the desert for a while without food and three days without water—but if you lose your faith and surrender to despair, you can't live for more than a few hours. Despair is deadly stuff. Faith, on the other hand, gives us something to live for, strive for, and work toward, and in which to see ourselves.

"Rabbi, I Just Can't Believe in the Jewish Idea of God."

My basic response to this is "Fine, but which God don't you believe in?" Usually, the skeptic starts telling me about the Old Man With a Beard Up in the Sky. I then gently suggest that the vast majority of Jews don't believe in that god, either. I certainly don't.

There are many "gods" that a Jew might not believe in. The Bible and the ancient rabbis believed in a highly personal God—a God Who made a covenant with the Jewish people and Who expected the Jewish people to fulfill that covenant through *mitzvot*, prayer, and Torah study. Jewish mystics believed in a God Who is imperfect, vulnerable, Whom we can get in touch with through intense meditation. The philosopher Baruch Spinoza, who lived in Amsterdam in the 1600s, believed in a God Who is part of the laws of nature. The modern German-Jewish thinker Martin Buber thought that God was revealed when people have deep relationships with each other. The modern thinker Mordecai Kaplan believed that God was the Power that assures our personal enhancement.

Whichever vision of God a Jew rejects or with which a Jew struggles, he or she is in good company. This is because Judaism has never had a strict list of beliefs that everyone had to accept. The essence of Judaism is not the idea of God. It is living *as if* there is a God. "Would that they deserted Me and kept My Torah," God says in the *midrash.* "For when they keep My Torah, that will be the way they come back to Me." In other words, even when you cannot believe in God, act *as if* there is a God in the world. Do Godly things. Study the words written by people who found themselves fired up with God's presence. We find God—and God finds us—when we live *as if* there is a God in the world.

One day in the early twentieth century, the great writer Franz Kafka was strolling in a park in Berlin. There he saw a little girl crying because she had lost her doll. Kafka tried to comfort her, telling her that the doll had merely gone on a trip, and that he had just seen the doll and had spoken to it. The doll had promised Kafka that it would stay in touch with the girl and would send a letter to her from time to time. Whenever she came to the park, Kafka said, he would bring her a letter from the doll.

So Kafka wrote letters to the little girl, and let her think that the doll had written them. Eventually, he sent her a new doll. He told her that the new doll was the old doll, but its appearance had changed since the last time she saw it because it had had such great adventures.

What does the doll represent? It symbolizes religious faith. The "old doll"—the religion of our ancestors—has indeed changed. But by struggling with our own faith, we can create a new belief for ourselves that is based on the solid foundations of what our ancestors built.

You May Be More Religious Than You Think

This past year, I was teaching my confirmation students about God. I wanted them to learn about some of the "proofs" that people have used for God's existence: nature is so vast and wonderful that it could not have created itself; or when people act decently and justly they are "listening" to the voice of conscience, which is really the voice of God.

We had not gotten very far in the discussion when a student raised her hand and asked, "Rabbi, I am writing a paper for school on religion. Am I supposed to write God's Name as 'G-d'?"

She was really asking a different question: How should God enter the everyday, "nonreligious" moments of my life? Do I have to bring God to school with me?

So I explained the origins of this writing of God's Name as "G-d." In the ancient Temple, the High Priest would enter the Holy of Holies on Yom Kippur and utter the Unpronounceable Four-Letter Name of God: *Yud Hey Vav Hey*. Over time, we lost the vowels for the name, and we forgot how to pronounce it. Ultimately, the Hebrew name of God became *Adonai*, and many Jews, even to this day, will not pronounce *Adonai* in nonreligious settings. They will only say *Ha-shem*, the Name—and they will write God's Name in Hebrew as simply *Hey*, the Hebrew letter at the beginning of *Ha-shem*. And they will spell God in English only as G-d. They also considered it to be religiously "impolite" to even try to pronounce *Yud Hey Vav Hey* as the Name of God.

A hand went up in my confirmation class. "What's wrong with saying God's Name?"

We talked about the meaning of holy speech and unholy speech—

about the differences between the way we talk with our friends and the way that we talk to God. We also talked about the ethics of speech, one rule of which is this: You don't have to say everything you know or that you think you know.

Then I asked the students, "Have there ever been times when you have felt the presence of the Unpronounceable Name of God?" The heads started to nod, and the stories started to flow. A young man described feeling God's Presence in nature. A young woman described feeling God when she stood over the Torah scroll at her bat mitzvah. Another young man talked about how he felt God's Presence when he was on a camping trip and got lost. Another young woman told us that she felt God's nearness when her grandmother died.

We talked about this for an hour and a half. And by the end, something had happened. Out of our own experiences, we were able to remember moments when we felt touched by something higher.

God was there with us.

★

What are some of the doubts that you have about Judaism, bar and bat mitzvah, faith, and God?

_____

When have you felt God's Presence? _____

When have you doubted God's Presence? _____

Does religion cause evil? What are the pros and cons of believing this?

_____

If you could create your own religion, what would it look like? What kinds of rituals would you include in it?

_____

Is it possible to "prove" God's existence? If you were going to try to convince someone that there is a God, what would you say?

_____

8

A Road Map to the Shabbat Morning Worship Service

FINDING YOUR PLACE IN THE WORDS

I do not understand
the book in my hand.

Who will teach me to return?
Loss of custom, ruin of will,
A memory of a memory
thinner than a vein.
Who will teach us to return? . . .

We do not want to come back.

We do not know where we are.

Not knowing where we are, how can we know
where we should go?

—Cynthia Ozick, "In the Synagogue"

I admit it: I know almost nothing about sports. When I watch the Super Bowl with friends, I have no idea what's going on. I don't know the names of the teams; I don't know the names of the players; I have no idea what the colors of the uniforms mean, or even why football players wear that little smudge of black stuff under their eyes. When it comes to football, I am hopeless.

There is something else I freely admit: I know almost nothing about ballet. You may not think that this is such a big deal, but in some places, knowing about ballet is very important. I admit that I do not know the stories of the major ballets, though I certainly admire the talent of the great ballet artists of our times. But when I go to the ballet (which is not very often), I have no idea what is going on.

That's the way it is in every Jewish congregation in North America. Many Jews are uncomfortable with Jewish worship. They act as I do when I watch the Super Bowl or when I go to a ballet: clueless.

In too many Shabbat morning bar and bat mitzvah services, guests arrive late. They come just in time for the Torah reading. And people don't seem to be praying. Sometimes they don't even open the prayer book. They often seem lost. They may even have no idea what the service is about. They don't know what to do, where to read, what to read, what page to turn to, when to stand, when to sit, when to sing.

What has happened? Too often, Jewish worshiping *congregations* have become *audiences*. Some people even say, "There were fifty people in the *audience* last Shabbat." This is not good. It turns cantors and rabbis into performers, or masters of ceremonies, or talk show hosts like Oprah.

Worship should inspire us. It should make us better, help us feel God's Presence, help us remember the covenant. People should pray with *kavvanah*, with sacred intention. They need to care about the words they are praying. They have to really be *there*. That is the meaning of the words that are often written over the *bimah*, the raised platform in the synagogue: *Da lifnei mi attah omed*, "know before Whom you stand." When Jews pray with *kavvanah*, they know that they stand before God.

What should true prayer be like? It should be like going to a Rolling Stones concert. I've been a Stones fan for more than forty years. Hearing Mick Jagger sing is like hearing an old friend. I know the old songs, and I can usually tell what song they are about to sing just by the introduction. That is what Jewish worship can be: knowing it all so well that the prayers resonate within our hearts.

Is a Worship Service "Theater"?

Think of the Shabbat morning service as *participatory theater*. What happens when you go to the theater? You watch a performance on a stage, complete with props, choreography, and gestures. The actors know the lines that they have learned from their scripts. The audience is passive and applauds the actors at appropriate times.

But what happens in the "theater" experience of the Shabbat morning service? There is also a script—a script that tells a story. As in the theater, the service has its own staging, props, movement, and script.

Take the *staging*, for example. Where participants in a service stand is very important. What's the most important place in the synagogue? Right before the Ark. In fact, the moment when a bar or bat mitzvah boy or girl stands before the Ark is the holiest moment of his or her life. Why is that? Because the Ark in the synagogue is not *just* the Ark in the synagogue. No—at that moment, the Ark is "really" the Ark in the ancient Temple, the holiest place in the world.

Take *props*, for example. The prayer book, in one sense, is a prop. So is the Torah scroll. The way we handle those props is very important. They must be handled with delicacy and with love. Take *movement*. We stand at the holiest moments of the service. We bow. We bend our knees. Some worshipers even jump up on their toes at certain points in the service, so they can feel as if they are flying up to the heavens.

Finally, the *script*.

Our script is the *siddur*, the Jewish prayer book. The word *siddur* comes from the Hebrew word "order." Things happen during a service in a certain *order*. The *siddur* was first compiled during the eight and ninth centuries C.E., though the basic form of the service and many prayers already existed by about 200 C.E., and even earlier for others.

The *siddur* is not just a script. It is much deeper and holier than that.

There is a wonderful story about a man who survived the Holocaust. When he entered Auschwitz, he was sure that he would survive, but he was also sure that he would be the last Jew on earth. He also believed that if that were true, it would be his job to rebuild Judaism, from the ground up.

But how would he do that? He decided to memorize the *siddur* prayer by prayer, even though he did not have one with him. He would play *siddur* "memory games" with other Jews in the camp to keep their minds alive. When he got out of the camp, he knew the entire *siddur*. "I am a living prayer book," he told his friends and community. More than that: He was living Judaism. For in a very real sense, the *siddur is* Judaism.

There are also *actors* in the Jewish service. All of us—the rabbi, the cantor, and everyone in the congregation—are the actors. We perform a sacred drama, one that reflects our beliefs, our needs, our dreams, our values.

And who is the *audience*? *God* is the audience, as well as being the main character. In fact, we are doing all this for God.

The Acts of the Script

So, we have a script—the *siddur*. And the script tells a story the way we Jewish people view the world. Every play is broken into "acts." The acts are the traditional sections of the worship service.

Act One is the *Shema* and its blessings. Beginning with the *Barechu*, we learn *what Jews believe:* God creates; God loves the Jewish people through Torah; God redeems the Jewish people from Egypt.

Act Two is *Tefilah*, or "prayer." It is also known as the *shemoneh esreh* (the eighteen prayers) or the *amidah* (the standing prayer) because it is traditionally recited while we stand. It talks about *what we need* as Jews: to be linked to our ancestors; to believe that there is a reality to us that goes beyond death; to feel part of God's Holiness; to give thanks; to find fulfillment and *shalom* (peace). This is the part of the service where we ask God for things for ourselves and for our people. There are many more requests in the daily *tefilah*—pleas for healing, sustenance, forgiveness, the restoration of Jerusalem. But we don't ask God for much during the Shabbat service. This is why: Shabbat is like the *coming attractions* of the Messianic Age. In the Messianic Age, we will not need much of anything.

Act Three is the Torah reading. It is *what we learn*. This act takes place on Mondays, Thursdays, festivals, Rosh Chodesh (the first day of the Jewish month), and of course, Shabbat. During this section of the service on Shabbat mornings, the *haftarah* is also read.

Act Four during the service is *what we hope*. It contains *Aleinu* and *Kaddish*—prayers in which we say that someday everyone will understand that God is One, and that someday there will be perfection and peace, God's Kingdom on earth.

These are the four basic acts of the worship service. Some synagogues also read introductory prayers, *Birchot Hashachar* ("the morning blessings") and *Pesukei Dezimra* ("verses of song"). In Conservative and Orthodox synagogues, an additional service, called *musaf*, corresponds with what was the additional sacrifice in the ancient Temple in Jerusalem and repeats some themes of the earlier liturgy. It is customarily recited after the Torah service.

Learning How to Pray Like a Pro

I am going to teach you the most important Jewish prayers and ask you to think of some things that are related to those prayers.

But you can't learn Jewish worship the way you learn a vocabulary list or the multiplication tables. There is only one way to truly learn the worship service. You have to pray it and sing it with a congregation. Anything else is like going to the theater. The music may sound good, but you can't sing along. This is why you need to attend services regularly during the year before (and, it goes without saying, after) your bar or bat mitzvah ceremony.

Barechu • Praise!

בָּרְכוּ אֶת־יְיָ הַמְבֹרָךְ!

בָּרוּךְ יְיָ הַמְבֹרָךְ לְעוֹלָם וָעֶד!

Praise Adonai, the Blessed One!
Praised be Adonai, Who is blessed forever!

Yotzer* • Creator

בָּרוּךְ אַתָּה, יְיָ אֱלֹהֵינוּ, מֶלֶךְ הָעוֹלָם, יוֹצֵר אוֹר וּבוֹרֵא חֹשֶׁךְ,
עֹשֶׂה שָׁלוֹם וּבוֹרֵא אֶת הַכֹּל. הַמֵּאִיר לָאָרֶץ וְלַדָּרִים עָלֶיהָ
בְּרַחֲמִים, וּבְטוּבוֹ מְחַדֵּשׁ בְּכָל־יוֹם תָּמִיד מַעֲשֵׂה בְרֵאשִׁית.

מָה רַבּוּ מַעֲשֶׂיךָ, יְיָ! כֻּלָּם בְּחָכְמָה עָשִׂיתָ, מָלְאָה הָאָרֶץ
קִנְיָנֶךָ. תִּתְבָּרַךְ, יְיָ אֱלֹהֵינוּ, עַל־שֶׁבַח מַעֲשֵׂה יָדֶיךָ, וְעַל־
מְאוֹרֵי־אוֹר שֶׁעָשִׂיתָ: יְפָאֲרוּךָ. סֶלָה. בָּרוּךְ אַתָּה, יְיָ,
יוֹצֵר הַמְּאוֹרוֹת.

Praised are You, Adonai our God, Ruler of the universe, who fashions light and creates darkness, who establishes peace and creates all things. You illumine the earth and all its inhabitants with compassion, and with goodness renew the work of creation daily.

How manifold are Your works, Adonai; You have made all of them in wisdom; Your creations fill the earth. You are praised, Adonai our God, for the splendor of the work of Your hands; and for the glowing lights that You have made, You are glorified forever. Praised are You, Adonai, the Creator of the lights.

---

*This is one of several versions of this prayer.

Yotzer is the morning prayer of creation. Its theme is the creation of light and darkness. It affirms that God creates and re-creates the world every day.

In Robert Fulghum's book *It Was on Fire When I Lay Down on It,* he tells the following story:

> During World War II, Nazi paratroopers who had invaded the island of Crete in the Mediterranean Sea were attacked by peasants wielding kitchen knives and farm tools. In retaliation, the population was rounded up, executed, and buried in a mass grave. Years later, in response to what he saw on Crete, Dr. Alexander Papaderos formed the Institute for Reconciliation, which is devoted to furthering human understanding. To remind himself of the meaning of life, Dr. Papaderos carries in his pocket a small, round piece of glass, no larger than a quarter. It is a piece of a mirror from a German motorcycle that as a small boy he had found shattered on the road. He used to delight in shining its reflective light into dark places where the sun would never shine, in deep holes and crevices and dark closets.
>
> "It became a game for me to get light into the most inaccessible places I could find," he said. "I kept the little mirror and as I went about growing up, I would take it out in idle moments and continue the challenge of the game. As I grew to manhood, I came to understand that this was not just a child's game, but actually a metaphor for what I might do with my life. I came to understand that I am not the light or the source of light. But the light is there, and it will only shine in the dark places if I choose to reflect it."

✦

How are you making light shine into the dark places in your life?

_____

How are you separating light from darkness?

_____

How have you felt a sense of creative
purpose operating in you and in the world? _____

Shema Yisrael · Hear, Israel!

שְׁמַע יִשְׂרָאֵל: יְיָ אֱלֹהֵינוּ, יְיָ אֶחָד!
בָּרוּךְ שֵׁם כְּבוֹד מַלְכוּתוֹ לְעוֹלָם וָעֶד!

Hear, O Israel: Adonai is our God, Adonai is one!
Blessed is the glorious realm of God for ever and ever!

Elie Wiesel tells of a group of Jews who wanted to celebrate *Simchat Torah* in a barracks at Auschwitz. But they lacked a Torah. An old man asked a young boy, "Do you remember what you learned in *cheder* [Jewish religious school]?"

"Yes, I do," replied the young boy.

"Really?" said the old man. "You really remember *Shema Yisrael*?"

"I remember much more," said the young boy.

"*Shema Yisrael* is enough," said the old man. And he lifted the boy from the ground and began dancing with him, as though he were the Torah.

"Never before," Wiesel later wrote, "had Jews celebrated *Simchat Torah* with such fervor."

That is the power of the *Shema*, and it is on our lips twice daily, morning and evening. The *Shema* has been on the lips of our martyrs. It has been on the lips of those who have sought strength. It has been on the lips of those who are about to depart from this world.

✦

What words do I live by in my life? _____

What words are important to me in my life?

_____

What does it truly mean for God to be One?

_____

How can I feel my life to be part of a larger, lasting Unity?

___

When have I felt connected to something beyond me?

___

 Ve-ahavta • You Shall Love . . .

וְאָהַבְתָּ אֵת יְיָ אֱלֹהֶיךָ בְּכָל־לְבָבְךָ וּבְכָל־נַפְשְׁךָ וּבְכָל־מְאֹדֶךָ.
וְהָיוּ הַדְּבָרִים הָאֵלֶּה, אֲשֶׁר אָנֹכִי מְצַוְּךָ הַיּוֹם, עַל־לְבָבֶךָ.
וְשִׁנַּנְתָּם לְבָנֶיךָ, וְדִבַּרְתָּ בָּם בְּשִׁבְתְּךָ בְּבֵיתֶךָ וּבְלֶכְתְּךָ
בַדֶּרֶךְ, וּבְשָׁכְבְּךָ וּבְקוּמֶךָ.

וּקְשַׁרְתָּם לְאוֹת עַל־יָדֶךָ, וְהָיוּ לְטֹטָפֹת בֵּין עֵינֶיךָ, וּכְתַבְתָּם
עַל־מְזֻזוֹת בֵּיתֶךָ, וּבִשְׁעָרֶיךָ.

לְמַעַן תִּזְכְּרוּ וַעֲשִׂיתֶם אֶת־כָּל־מִצְוֹתָי, וִהְיִיתֶם קְדֹשִׁים
לֵאלֹהֵיכֶם. אֲנִי יְיָ אֱלֹהֵיכֶם, אֲשֶׁר הוֹצֵאתִי אֶתְכֶם מֵאֶרֶץ
מִצְרַיִם לִהְיוֹת לָכֶם לֵאלֹהִים. אֲנִי יְיָ אֱלֹהֵיכֶם.

You shall love Adonai your God with all your heart, with all
your soul, and with all your might. These words, which I
command you this day, shall be upon your heart. Teach
them faithfully to your children; speak of them in your
home and on your way, when you lie down and when you
rise up. Bind them as a sign upon your hand; let them be
symbols before your eyes; inscribe them on the doorposts
of your house, and on your gates. Thus may you remember
all of My *mitzvot,* and do them, and so consecrate your-
selves to your God. I, Adonai, am your God Who led you out
of Egypt to be your God; I, Adonai, am your God.

Ve-ahavta, which is part of the *Shema* unit, immediately follows the
Shema in the service (as well as in Deuteronomy 6), and it is also called
kabbalat ol hamitzvot ("the acceptance of the yoke of the *mitzvot*"). The

Ve-ahavta tells us that it's not enough to know that there is a God. We have to make that knowledge come alive through specific actions.

What actions?

"Teach them to your children." You are learning Judaism. And while it might be very hard to even imagine this, someday you might have children. Make sure you teach them Judaism as well.

"Speak of them in your home and on your way, when you lie down and when you rise up." Judaism does not just "live" in the synagogue. You can take Judaism into the world with you. Have you ever thought about how Judaism affects the way you treat your parents, or your teachers, or other kids?

"Bind them as a sign upon your hand; let them be symbols before your eyes." This is why many Jews wear *tefilin* (the leather boxes that contain words of Torah and that are worn on the forearm and on the forehead). The *tefilin* are worn during the weekday morning service. We wear them between our eyes so that Torah becomes our way of seeing the world. We wear them on our arms so that Torah teaches us how to *act* in the world. The *tefilin* on the arm face the heart, so that Torah will be inside us.

"Inscribe them on the doorposts of your house and on your gates." This is why Jews have a *mezuzah* on the doorposts of their homes. The doorpost is an interesting place. It is where the outside world meets the inside world.

Can you imagine what it is to love God "with all your heart"?

How are you bringing God into your home? To school with you? To play with you? Into the world?

Geulah · Redemption

אֱמֶת וְיַצִּיב, וְאָהוּב וְחָבִיב, וְנוֹרָא וְאַדִּיר, וְטוֹב וְיָפֶה הַדָּבָר
הַזֶּה עָלֵינוּ לְעוֹלָם וָעֶד. אֱמֶת, אֱלֹהֵי עוֹלָם מַלְכֵּנוּ, צוּר יַעֲקֹב
מָגֵן יִשְׁעֵנוּ.

לְדֹר וָדֹר הוּא קַיָּם, וּשְׁמוֹ קַיָּם, וְכִסְאוֹ נָכוֹן, וּמַלְכוּתוֹ
וֶאֱמוּנָתוֹ לָעַד קַיֶּמֶת. וּדְבָרָיו חָיִים וְקַיָּמִים, נֶאֱמָנִים
וְנֶחֱמָדִים, לָעַד וּלְעוֹלְמֵי עוֹלָמִים.

מִמִּצְרַיִם גְּאַלְתָּנוּ, יְיָ אֱלֹהֵינוּ, וּמִבֵּית עֲבָדִים פְּדִיתָנוּ.

עַל־זֹאת שִׁבְּחוּ אֲהוּבִים וְרוֹמְמוּ אֵל, וְנָתְנוּ יְדִידִים זְמִירוֹת,
שִׁירוֹת וְתִשְׁבָּחוֹת, בְּרָכוֹת וְהוֹדָאוֹת לַמֶּלֶךְ, אֵל חַי וְקַיָּם.

רָם וְנִשָּׂא, גָּדוֹל וְנוֹרָא, מַשְׁפִּיל גֵּאִים וּמַגְבִּיהַּ שְׁפָלִים, מוֹצִיא
אֲסִירִים וּפוֹדֶה עֲנָוִים, וְעוֹזֵר דַּלִּים, וְעוֹנֶה לְעַמּוֹ בְּעֵת שַׁוְּעָם
אֵלָיו.

מִי־כָמֹכָה בָּאֵלִם, יְיָ!

מִי כָּמֹכָה, נֶאְדָּר בַּקֹּדֶשׁ,

נוֹרָא תְהִלֹּת, עֹשֵׂה פֶלֶא!

שִׁירָה חֲדָשָׁה שִׁבְּחוּ גְאוּלִים לְשִׁמְךָ עַל־שְׂפַת הַיָּם. יַחַד כֻּלָּם
הוֹדוּ וְהִמְלִיכוּ וְאָמְרוּ: יְיָ יִמְלֹךְ לְעוֹלָם וָעֶד.

צוּר יִשְׂרָאֵל, קוּמָה בְּעֶזְרַת יִשְׂרָאֵל, וּפְדֵה כִנְאֻמֶךָ יְהוּדָה
וְיִשְׂרָאֵל. גֹּאֲלֵנוּ, יְיָ צְבָאוֹת שְׁמוֹ, קְדוֹשׁ יִשְׂרָאֵל. בָּרוּךְ אַתָּה,
יְיָ, גָּאַל יִשְׂרָאֵל.

This will for ever be true and everlasting, beloved and precious, awesome, powerful, good and beautiful for us: The Eternal God truly is our Sovereign, the Rock of Jacob our protecting Shield.

You endure from generation to generation, as Your name

endures; Your throne remains, as Your sovereignty and faithfulness abide forever.

Your words live and endure, forever a precious part of our faith, now and to all eternity.

You redeemed us from Egypt, Adonai our God, and set us free from the house of bondage.

For this Your beloved people praised and exalted God; Your precious people rendered melodies, songs, and praises, prayers and thanks to the Ruler, the living and eternal God.

You who are high and exalted, great and awesome, who can raise the valleys and lower the mountains, O free the captive and redeem the oppressed, and answer Your people when they cry out to You.

Who is like You among the gods, Adonai!

Who is like You, adorned with holiness, awesome in splendor, doing wonders!

Your children witnessed Your sovereignty as You parted the sea before Moses. "This is my God!" they exclaimed. "Adonai will reign for ever and ever!"

For as it has been said: "Adonai delivered Jacob, redeeming him from the hand of an overpowering aggressor." Praised are You, Adonai, the Redeemer of Israel.

The *Geulah* prayer speaks of how we were freed (redeemed) from Egypt. It climaxes with the triumphant singing of *Mi Chamocha*: "Who is like you, among the gods, *Adonai?*" Moses and the Israelites sang this song at the shores of the Sea of Reeds.

As we sing *Mi Chamocha*, we try to imagine walking through the parted waters of the Sea. A Hasidic sect marks the last day of Pesach by pouring gallons of water on the floor of the synagogue so worshipers can walk through it and relive the experience of the Sea.

✦

How have you helped those seeking freedom?

 Avot · Fathers or Ancestors

בָּרוּךְ אַתָּה, יְיָ אֱלֹהֵינוּ וֵאלֹהֵי אֲבוֹתֵינוּ, אֱלֹהֵי אַבְרָהָם, אֱלֹהֵי
יִצְחָק, וֵאלֹהֵי יַעֲקֹב הָאֵל הַגָּדוֹל, הַגִּבּוֹר וְהַנּוֹרָא, אֵל עֶלְיוֹן.
גּוֹמֵל חֲסָדִים טוֹבִים, וְקוֹנֵה הַכֹּל, וְזוֹכֵר חַסְדֵי אָבוֹת, וּמֵבִיא
גְאֻלָּה לִבְנֵי בְנֵיהֶם, לְמַעַן שְׁמוֹ, בְּאַהֲבָה.
מֶלֶךְ עוֹזֵר וּמוֹשִׁיעַ וּמָגֵן. בָּרוּךְ אַתָּה, יְיָ, מָגֵן אַבְרָהָם.

Praised are You, Adonai our God and God of our ancestors:
God of Abraham, God of Isaac, God of Jacob; great, mighty,
and awesome God, God supreme. [Some versions: Praised
are You, Adonai our God and God of our ancestors: God of
Abraham, God of Isaac, God of Jacob; God of Sarah, God of
Rebecca, God of Rachel and God of Leah.]

Grantor of love and kindness, You care for us all by remembering the devotion of our ancestors, and in love, bringing
redemption to their descendants for the sake of Your name.

Our Ruler helps and saves and protects us. Praised are You,
Adonai, the Protector of Abraham (*some versions:* "and the
helper of Sarah").

The *Avot* prayer connects us to our ancestors. They had a faith, a way
of life, a way of standing up to overwhelming odds, each with their
own relationship with God.

    Avot is not only about Abraham and Sarah, Isaac and Rebecca,
Jacob and Rachel and Leah. It's about praying to the God of your parents and your grandparents and your great-grandparents. You are

praying all the way back into history. Praying is not only speaking to God. Praying is remembering that all the generations of the Jewish people are connected to God in a living covenant. But notice something. The prayer says: "*God* of Abraham, *God* of Isaac, and *God* of Jacob." It does not state: "God of Abraham, Isaac, and Jacob." As the Jewish thinker Martin Buber noted, every generation must come to its own idea of God. Our way of looking at God may be different from our parents'. It may be different from our grandparents'. Yet, we are all part of the same people and the same religion.

✦

What have your parents taught you about God?

_____

What have your grandparents taught you about God?

_____

 Gevurot • Powers

אַתָּה גִּבּוֹר לְעוֹלָם, אֲדֹנָי, מְחַיֵּה הַכֹּל אַתָּה, רַב לְהוֹשִׁיעַ.
מְכַלְכֵּל חַיִּים בְּחֶסֶד, מְחַיֵּה הַכֹּל בְּרַחֲמִים רַבִּים. סוֹמֵךְ
נוֹפְלִים, וְרוֹפֵא חוֹלִים, וּמַתִּיר אֲסוּרִים, וּמְקַיֵּם אֱמוּנָתוֹ
לִישֵׁנֵי עָפָר.

מִי כָמוֹךָ בַּעַל גְּבוּרוֹת, וּמִי דוֹמֶה לָּךְ, מֶלֶךְ מֵמִית וּמְחַיֵּה
וּמַצְמִיחַ יְשׁוּעָה.

וְנֶאֱמָן אַתָּה לְהַחֲיוֹת הַכֹּל. בָּרוּךְ אַתָּה, יְיָ, מְחַיֵּה הַכֹּל.

Eternal is Your power, Adonai, giving life to all [or, traditionally, "giving life to the dead"] through magnificent salvation. With faithful love, You sustain the living, and with great compassion give life to all. You support the fallen and heal the sick, free the captive and keep faith with those who sleep in the dust.

Who is like You, Master of Might, and who can compare to
You, our Sovereign, Who rules death and life, causing salvation to flourish!

You faithfully give life to all. Praised are You, Adonai, Who
gives life to all [or, traditionally, "who gives life to the
dead"].

Most people don't think about death. If they do, they don't think about
it very often. But it's true: Judaism believes in some kind of life after
death. Some Jews believe that the soul is immortal—that all the good
things that we did will survive forever. I feel that way about some of
my teachers and rabbis: they may be dead, but what they taught me
will live forever. Maybe you have a grandparent or another close family member who has died. If so, you probably sense that they are still
"with" you in many ways. Traditional Jews believe that in the Messianic Age, the dead will come back to life, and be "resurrected." That
is why, for example, traditional Jews frown on autopsies—they don't
want anything to happen that would violate the body of the dead person. That is also why traditional versions of the *Gevurot* prayer speak
of God as *mechayeh hametim* ("the One who resurrects the dead").
Reform versions speak of God as *mechayeh hakol* ("Who gives life to
all"), since Reform Judaism historically does not believe in resurrection.

All this basically means that God has given us the power to hope,
that something non-physical and beyond our bodies lives forever. We
call that non-physical "something" the soul. Because we have souls,
we are endowed with eternal worth and eternal hope.

Here's a story about that. In 1962, an Israeli submarine sank off
the coast of Israel. All the sailors were drowned. Soon after, the father
of one of the sailors attended a basketball game that his son's old team
won. "When my son comes back, I will tell him of your victory," he
said to his son's old teammates. Was the old man crazy? Had he somehow *forgotten* that his son was dead? Absolutely not. He knew that his
son was dead. But still there was that hope that someday. . . .

Hope is even stronger than death.

✦

Have you ever felt the presence of a loved one who has died?

_____

What do you hope for? _____

Are there times when you have sensed
that hope is even stronger than death? _____

 Kedusha · Sanctification

נְקַדֵּשׁ אֶת־שִׁמְךָ בָּעוֹלָם, כְּשֵׁם שֶׁמַּקְדִּישִׁים אוֹתוֹ בִּשְׁמֵי מָרוֹם,
כַּכָּתוּב עַל־יַד נְבִיאֶךָ: וְקָרָא זֶה אֶל־זֶה וְאָמַר:

קָדוֹשׁ, קָדוֹשׁ, קָדוֹשׁ יְיָ צְבָאוֹת, מְלֹא כָל־הָאָרֶץ כְּבוֹדוֹ.

לְעֻמָּתָם בָּרוּךְ יֹאמֵרוּ:

בָּרוּךְ כְּבוֹד יְיָ מִמְּקוֹמוֹ.

וּבְדִבְרֵי קָדְשְׁךָ כָּתוּב לֵאמֹר:

יִמְלֹךְ יְיָ לְעוֹלָם, אֱלֹהַיִךְ צִיּוֹן, לְדֹר וָדֹר, הַלְלוּיָהּ.

לְדוֹר וָדוֹר נַגִּיד גָּדְלֶךָ, וּלְנֵצַח נְצָחִים קְדֻשָּׁתְךָ נַקְדִּישׁ.
וְשִׁבְחֲךָ, אֱלֹהֵינוּ, מִפִּינוּ לֹא יָמוּשׁ לְעוֹלָם וָעֶד. בָּרוּךְ אַתָּה,
יְיָ, הָאֵל הַקָּדוֹשׁ.

Let us proclaim the sanctity of Your name here on earth,
just as it is proclaimed in the high heavens; as recorded by
Your prophet, let us cry out one to another:
Holy, Holy, Holy is Adonai of Hosts; the fullness of the
whole earth is God's glory!

We respond with blessing:
Blessed be God's seat of glory!

Following Your sacred words we say:

Adonai shall reign forever, your God, O Zion, from generation to generation. Halleluyah!

From generation to generation we will tell of Your greatness, and to the ends of time proclaim Your holiness. Your
praise, O God, shall never leave our lips. Praised are You,
Adonai, the holy God.

The *Kedusha* is best known by the refrain *Kadosh kadosh kadosh Adonai
zevaot, melo kol haaretz kevodo:* "Holy, holy, holy is the Lord of Hosts.
The whole earth is full of God's glory." It is the prophet Isaiah's vision
of the angelic beings that surround the Divine Throne (Isaiah 6:3). This
is the part of the service when some worshipers go up on their toes, as
if they were flying toward the Divine Throne. Yes, we believe that God
is everywhere, but most of us believe that we should always try to
ascend higher and higher.

✦

When have you felt spiritually elevated and inspired?

_____

What are those moments when you felt that God was close to you?

_____

 Kedushat Ha-Yom • Sanctification of the Day

Yismechu

יִשְׂמְחוּ בְמַלְכוּתְךָ שׁוֹמְרֵי שַׁבָּת וְקוֹרְאֵי עֹנֶג. עַם מְקַדְּשֵׁי
שְׁבִיעִי כֻּלָּם יִשְׂבְּעוּ וְיִתְעַנְּגוּ מִטּוּבֶךָ. וְהַשְּׁבִיעִי רָצִיתָ בּוֹ
וְקִדַּשְׁתּוֹ. חֶמְדַּת יָמִים אוֹתוֹ קָרָאתָ זֵכֶר לְמַעֲשֵׂה בְרֵאשִׁית.

Those who keep Shabbat and call it a delight shall rejoice in
Your reign. The nation that keeps the seventh day holy shall

be delighted by Your goodness. For you favored the seventh day and sanctified it, calling it the most precious of days, a memory of the act of creation.

Veshamru

וְשָׁמְרוּ בְנֵי־יִשְׂרָאֵל אֶת הַשַּׁבָּת, לַעֲשׂוֹת אֶת־הַשַּׁבָּת לְדֹרֹתָם בְּרִית עוֹלָם. בֵּינִי וּבֵין בְּנֵי יִשְׂרָאֵל אוֹת הִיא לְעֹלָם, כִּי שֵׁשֶׁת יָמִים עָשָׂה יְיָ אֶת־הַשָּׁמַיִם וְאֶת־הָאָרֶץ, וּבַיּוֹם הַשְּׁבִיעִי שָׁבַת וַיִּנָּפַשׁ.

The people of Israel shall keep Shabbat, observing Shabbat throughout all their generations as an eternal covenant. It is a sign between Me and the people of Israel for ever, because in six days Adonai created the heavens and earth, and on the seventh day ceased from work and rested.

Our God and God of our ancestors, favor our rest. Sanctify us with Your commandments and let us share in Your Torah. Satisfy us with Your goodness, gladden us with Your salvation, and purify our hearts to serve You in truth. Adonai our God, in Your gracious love let Your holy Sabbath be our heritage, that in it all of Israel, hallowing Your name, may find rest. Praised are You, Adonai, who sanctifies the Sabbath.

Kedushat Ha-Yom sanctifies the Shabbat day, through the singing of either *Yismechu* or *Veshamru*. We link God's holiness to the holiness of this moment in Jewish time.

✦

What are the holiest moments in your life?

_____

How have you made Shabbat a holy time?

_____

Avodah • Worship

רְצֵה, יְיָ אֱלֹהֵינוּ, בְּעַמְּךָ יִשְׂרָאֵל, וּתְפִלָּתָם בְּאַהֲבָה תְקַבֵּל, וּתְהִי לְרָצוֹן תָּמִיד עֲבוֹדַת יִשְׂרָאֵל עַמֶּךָ. אֵל קָרוֹב לְכָל־ קֹרְאָיו, פְּנֵה אֶל עֲבָדֶיךָ וְחָנֵּנוּ. שְׁפוֹךְ רוּחֲךָ עָלֵינוּ, וְתֶחֱזֶינָה עֵינֵינוּ בְּשׁוּבְךָ לְצִיּוֹן בְּרַחֲמִים.

בָּרוּךְ אַתָּה, יְיָ, הַמַּחֲזִיר שְׁכִינָתוֹ לְצִיּוֹן.

Take pleasure, Adonai our God, in Your people Israel, and accept our prayer with love. May our worship always be acceptable to You. God is close to all who call; turn to Your servants and be gracious to us. Pour out Your spirit upon us, and may our eyes behold Your return to Zion in compassion. Praised are You, Adonai, Who returns the wandering indwelling Divine Presence to Zion.

Avodah focuses our attention on a distant part of our history: the sacrificial offerings in the ancient Temple in Jerusalem. We also remember that although we no longer have a Temple, every Jewish home is a *mikdash m'at* (a "miniature sanctuary") in which the ordinary can be transformed into the sacred. For example, dinner on Thursday night might be a simple take-out pizza, eaten on paper plates. But on Shabbat, the table can be set with good china, and dinner can be special and holy.

I love this prayer, especially its *chatimah* (the "closing" or the "sealing" of the prayer). This is my own translation: "Blessed is Adonai, who returns the wandering Presence of God to Zion." I always say that prayer when I first see Israel's shoreline from the descending El Al jetliner. We live in a time in which Jews have come home to Israel. In coming home to Israel, we have learned that God has not abandoned our people. Some sages say that God's Presence was in exile with us. If that is true, then God has returned with us to Zion, the Land of Israel.

✦

What might it feel like to bring an offering to prayer?

_____

What would your offering be? _____

How can you create holy places in your life?

_____

Have you had an especially moving experience in Israel?

_____

How is the Land of Israel holy to Jews? _____

 Hodaah · Thanksgiving

מוֹדִים אֲנַחְנוּ לָךְ, שָׁאַתָּה הוּא יְיָ אֱלֹהֵינוּ וֵאלֹהֵי אֲבוֹתֵינוּ
לְעוֹלָם וָעֶד. צוּר חַיֵּינוּ, מָגֵן יִשְׁעֵנוּ, אַתָּה הוּא לְדוֹר וָדוֹר.
נוֹדֶה לְךָ וּנְסַפֵּר תְּהִלָּתֶךָ, עַל־חַיֵּינוּ הַמְּסוּרִים בְּיָדֶךָ, וְעַל־
נִשְׁמוֹתֵינוּ הַפְּקוּדוֹת לָךְ, וְעַל־נִסֶּיךָ שֶׁבְּכָל־יוֹם עִמָּנוּ, וְעַל־
נִפְלְאוֹתֶיךָ וְטוֹבוֹתֶיךָ שֶׁבְּכָל־עֵת, עֶרֶב וָבֹקֶר וְצָהֳרָיִם. הַטּוֹב
כִּי לֹא־כָלוּ רַחֲמֶיךָ, וְהַמְרַחֵם: כִּי־לֹא תַמּוּ חֲסָדֶיךָ, מֵעוֹלָם
קִוִּינוּ לָךְ.

וְעַל כֻּלָּם יִתְבָּרַךְ וְיִתְרוֹמַם שִׁמְךָ, מַלְכֵּנוּ, תָּמִיד לְעוֹלָם וָעֶד.

We acknowledge that You are Adonai our God and the God
of our ancestors, forever. You are the Rock of our life, our
Protector in salvation from generation to generation. And so
we thank You and sing Your praises, for our lives which are
in Your hand; and for our souls, which are entrusted to You;
for Your miracles which are among us daily; and for Your
wondrous and great acts of every hour, morning, noon, and
night. You are beneficent, for Your mercy is unending; You
are merciful, for Your love is unending. You have always
been our hope.

For all these things, our Ruler, may Your name be blessed and exalted, for ever and ever.

Hodaah asks us to remember to be thankful for what we have. Because it is Shabbat, there is little that we ask of God. Shabbat is a dress rehearsal for Messianic times, the time when the Messiah will come, giving us the opportunity to imagine what life would be like without asking for anything, to have all our needs satisfied. We give thanks for all that we have, for all that we might have, for the ability to give thanks. (This is why the very first thing you should do, on the Monday afternoon after your bar or bat mitzvah, is get started on those thank-you notes!)

✦

For what are you particularly grateful? _____

 Birchat Shalom • The Blessing of Peace

שִׂים שָׁלוֹם, טוֹבָה וּבְרָכָה, חֵן וָחֶסֶד וְרַחֲמִים, עָלֵינוּ וְעַל־כָּל־יִשְׂרָאֵל עַמֶּךָ.

Grant peace, goodness and blessing, grace, love, and mercy, for us, and for all of Israel, Your people.

Birchat Shalom reminds us that there is one thing that we do not have: peace. It calls for an end to violence, war, and bloodshed. Some versions of the prayer ask for peace not only for the Jewish people but for all the nations of the world as well. We remember that the accurate translation of *shalom* is not simply "peace," but "completeness," "fulfillment," and "wholeness."

✦

What are you doing to bring *shalom* into the world?

_____

Into your family? _____

Into your life? _____

What would give you a true sense of fulfillment and completeness?

_____

 Aleinu · It Is Incumbent upon Us

עָלֵינוּ לְשַׁבֵּחַ לַאֲדוֹן הַכֹּל, לָתֵת גְּדֻלָּה לְיוֹצֵר בְּרֵאשִׁית,
שֶׁלֹּא עָשָׂנוּ כְּגוֹיֵי הָאֲרָצוֹת, וְלֹא שָׂמָנוּ כְּמִשְׁפְּחוֹת הָאֲדָמָה,
שֶׁלֹּא שָׂם חֶלְקֵנוּ כָּהֶם, וְגֹרָלֵנוּ כְּכָל־הֲמוֹנָם.
וַאֲנַחְנוּ כּוֹרְעִים וּמִשְׁתַּחֲוִים וּמוֹדִים לִפְנֵי מֶלֶךְ מַלְכֵי
הַמְּלָכִים, הַקָּדוֹשׁ בָּרוּךְ הוּא.

We must praise the Master of all, ascribing greatness to the Creator, who has not made us like the nations of the world by giving us a unique portion and destiny.

So we humbly bow down in acknowledgment before the supreme Ruler of rulers, the Holy One of Blessing.

Some people just don't like *Aleinu*, which means "It is incumbent upon us." They don't like the line: "[God] has not made us like the nations of the world." This is probably the most misunderstood verse in Jewish prayer. In the late Middle Ages, some gentile rulers actually forbade Jews from singing it in their synagogues, believing that it insulted Christians. Actually the phrase "who has not made us like the nations of the world" means that God chose us for a unique task: to teach Torah to the world and to bring the world closer to a belief in the One God.

How do we do that? *Letakein olam bemalchut shaddai*, "repairing the world in the image of God's rule." To bring the world closer to how we sense God wants it to be. Our tools for doing this are the *mitzvot*.

✶

How are you trying to repair the world? _____

How are you bringing the day when
the world will reflect the Divine Unity? _____

 Mourners' Kaddish • Sanctification

יִתְגַּדַּל וְיִתְקַדַּשׁ שְׁמֵהּ רַבָּא בְּעָלְמָא דִּי־בְרָא כִרְעוּתֵהּ,
וְיַמְלִיךְ מַלְכוּתֵהּ בְּחַיֵּיכוֹן וּבְיוֹמֵיכוֹן וּבְחַיֵּי דְכָל־בֵּית
יִשְׂרָאֵל, בַּעֲגָלָא וּבִזְמַן קָרִיב, וְאִמְרוּ: אָמֵן.

יְהֵא שְׁמֵהּ רַבָּא מְבָרַךְ לְעָלַם וּלְעָלְמֵי עָלְמַיָּא!

יִתְבָּרַךְ וְיִשְׁתַּבַּח, וְיִתְפָּאַר וְיִתְרוֹמַם וְיִתְנַשֵּׂא, וְיִתְהַדָּר
וְיִתְעַלֶּה וְיִתְהַלָּל שְׁמֵהּ דְּקוּדְשָׁא, בְּרִיךְ הוּא, לְעֵלָּא מִן־
כָּל־בִּרְכָתָא וְשִׁירָתָא, תֻּשְׁבְּחָתָא וְנֶחֱמָתָא דַּאֲמִירָן בְּעָלְמָא,
וְאִמְרוּ: אָמֵן.

יְהֵא שְׁלָמָא רַבָּא מִן־שְׁמַיָּא וְחַיִּים עָלֵינוּ וְעַל־כָּל־יִשְׂרָאֵל
וְאִמְרוּ: אָמֵן.

עֹשֶׂה שָׁלוֹם בִּמְרוֹמָיו, הוּא יַעֲשֶׂה שָׁלוֹם עָלֵינוּ וְעַל־כָּל־
יִשְׂרָאֵל, וְאִמְרוּ: אָמֵן.

May Your great name be magnified and hallowed, in the
world created according to Your will, and may Your reign be
quickly established, in our own lives and our own day, and
in the life of all of Israel, and let us say: Amen.

May Your great name be blessed for ever and ever!

All praise and glory, splendor, exaltation and honor, radiance
and veneration and worship to the Holy One of Blessing,
even beyond any earthly prayer or song, any adoration or
tribute we can offer, and let us say: Amen.

May there be great peace from the heavens, and life for us
and for all of Israel, as we say: Amen.

> May the one who makes peace in the high heavens send peace for us and for all of Israel, as we say: Amen.

Finally, there is *Kaddish* ("sanctification"). *Kaddish* is a prayer in Aramaic, Hebrew's sister language. There are several different versions of *Kaddish*. But the version that most people know is the one we use as a mourners' prayer.

Kaddish never mentions death. It dreams of God's Kingdom, a time of perfection when death itself will disappear.

★

What do you have that has been left to you by someone you love?

_____

_____

_____

What prayers in the service do you find most meaningful? What particular meanings do you associate with them? How would you turn your feelings about bar and bat mitzvah into a prayer?

_____

_____

_____

9

After the Thank-You Notes

LIFE AFTER BAR AND BAT MITZVAH

Let young people . . . be sure that every deed counts,
that every word has power, and that we all can do
our share to redeem the world in spite of all its absurdities
and frustrations and disappointments. . . . Let them
remember to build a life as if it were a work of art.

—Abraham Joshua Heschel

Now that the ceremony is over, now that the photocopied sheets of Torah and *haftarah* are buried under your basketball and music magazines, now that the thank-you notes are finally written—what now? What does it really mean to go from Jewish childhood to Jewish adolescence—and ultimately to Jewish adulthood?

Remember That Judaism Teaches Different Truths

Look at the messages that the world sometimes sends us. "You are what you own." "The world owes me everything." "I deserve what I got, and those that don't 'got' don't deserve it, anyway."

All these messages are wrong because they can lead to idolatry: the worship of achievement, and things, and status. These things are wrong because they can ruin our relationships with other people and with God.

Consider the values that our people have taught over the centuries.

The world says, "Me first." Yet, Jewish tradition teaches *gemilut chasadim* (acts of loving-kindness). Judaism teaches us to give to others. Yet, too many people now give minimally or with a bad attitude to charity. Judaism says that charity is done because it is the path to justice. It is what we must do as part of our covenant with God.

Ours is a disposable fast-food world of Happy Meals, Coke, and styrofoam. Yet, Jewish tradition teaches the beauty of *challah* and wine on Shabbat, served on the best china on a dining room table covered with the whitest of white tablecloths. We do this to bring honor to Shabbat. Suddenly, the table is no longer *just* a table. It is a *mikdash m'at*, a sanctuary in miniature, a memory of the ancient Temple in Jerusalem. It is in *our* home. And it transforms *us*.

Our world has turned communication into gossip. Yet, Judaism teaches that the most beautiful words we can utter are words of *tefilah*, of prayer, and of the sacred learning of Torah.

Our world says that memories are rarely permanent. It is an insult to say to someone, "Hey, you're *history*." But Judaism teaches that memory is the path to holiness.

Our world believes that you can put information on a computer disc and give truth in sound bites. Yet, Judaism teaches ancient wisdom from a scroll that one person wrote painstakingly by hand.

Probably everyone is telling you that success and achievement in secular school are the most important thing in your life. There is good reason for this. You must do well in school in order to get into a good college, and therefore to do well in life.

But, in fact, here is the truth: You will ultimately "use" what you learn in religious school as much as—maybe even *more* than—you will use what you learn in regular school. You will use your knowledge of Shabbat customs, the meaning of Pesach, and the correct pronunciation of the Torah blessings and *Kaddish* far more than, say, geometry, European history, and the minerals of Bolivia. You will certainly call upon the values of Judaism—the values of honesty and truth and faithfulness and compassion and social justice—far more than much of what you will learn in public school.

This does not mean that it is OK to do poorly in "regular" school. Far from it! It just means that as your life unfolds, don't be surprised if you discover that Jewish learning is more important and life shaping than you had ever thought.

Continue Your Jewish Education

Every Saturday morning, week after week, in synagogues all over America, thirteen-year-olds are making beautiful speeches about Jewish responsibility, the value of Jewish learning, and the importance of the synagogue.

And yet, by the same time next week, or shortly thereafter, many of those young people are *gone*—missing in action. In 1987–1988, which is the last year for which research was done, the Institute of Contemporary Jewry at Hebrew University noted that while about eighty percent of all Jewish children were enrolled in Jewish education, after bar and bat mitzvah that figure fell to almost fifty percent. Jewish education after the bar and bat mitzvah is a major American Jewish problem.

And yet, bar and bat mitzvah was never intended to be the end of Jewish education. Reform Judaism contributed the idea of confirmation to the Jewish life cycle. Confirmation is a group ceremony that occurs when young people are in their early teens. (Depending on the community, it can be in ninth, tenth, or eleventh grade). The ceremony is usually held on Shavuot, the festival in late spring that commemorates the giving of the Torah. This is a wonderful experience—building a real sense of connection to the Jewish community and to Jewish learning.

Going on to confirmation—or beyond, to Hebrew high school— helps eliminate a special illness that many thirteen-year-old youngsters experience. Imagine the feeling: You go through a rigorous process with a wonderful, memorable ceremony—and then you feel something called "post-bar/bat mitzvah letdown." Is bar or bat mitzvah all there is to Judaism, you wonder.

But the age of thirteen is far too young for you to end your

Jewish education. Here are the top seven reasons why you should continue your Jewish education:

1. Rituals should mean what we say they mean. The ancient rabbis believed that young people develop a conscience no later than their thirteenth year. "Bar mitzvah" or "bat mitzvah" means, then, someone who is "old enough to have a conscience." And "conscience" means telling the truth. You *do* believe that Judaism is important. That is why you were bar or bat mitzvah. And you might as well live out that truth.

2. You need much more Jewish knowledge and wisdom if you are going to be a Jewish adult. A boy who was about to become bar mitzvah told me he wasn't sure that he wanted to continue his Jewish education. I finally asked him that dreaded question: "What are you thinking of doing when you grow up?"

He replied, "I want to go into the computer business."

"OK, then," I replied. "Here's the deal. In twenty years, you're going to want a job in the computer business. Some successor to Bill Gates is going to interview you."

"'What do you know about computers?' you'll be asked.

"'Well,' you'll say, 'I haven't turned on a computer since I was a teenager.' You won't get the job. Do you see what I mean?" I asked the boy. "If you're planning to be Jewish for the rest of your life, you should at least stay current with what's going on."

Of his Jewish childhood, actor Kirk Douglas recalled,

> No rational adult would make a business decision based on what they knew when they were fourteen. You wouldn't decide who to marry based on what you knew about love and relationships when you were fourteen. But lots of us seem satisfied to dismiss religion based on what we learned at fourteen, and I was one of those who was that stupid.

3. You have a responsibility to the Jewish community. You may not be thinking about this now, but what if everyone dropped out after bar or bat mitzvah? We would have a very ignorant, unconnected, unattractive Jewish community.

"Who cares?" you may ask. "Whatever I choose to do is my business."

Yes, but . . .

The ancient sages told a story about two men traveling together in a row boat. In the middle of the voyage, one of the men took out a drill and began to drill beneath his seat.

"What are you doing?!" his companion screamed. "Do you want to drown us?!"

"But I am only drilling under *my* seat, not yours!" the other man retorted.

Sorry. It doesn't work that way. We Jews are all voyagers on the same boat. That boat is called "The Jewish Future." If too many of us drill under our own seats, it will sink for everyone.

4. The Jewish future depends on educated Jews. The only way that Judaism survived this long was by having literate, informed Jews. We need our tradition for spiritual sustenance and moral nourishment.

I once heard the father of a young man who was becoming bar mitzvah bless him with these bittersweet words: "May I be the last ignorant Jew in this family."

5. You could learn something that will make a difference in your life. A nineteen-year-old visited me in my office several months ago. He was on his way to keep another appointment—to get a tattoo. "Rabbi," he asked me, "is it true that I can't be buried in a Jewish cemetery if I have a tattoo?"

The "no tattoos in a Jewish cemetery" rule is an interesting piece of American Jewish folklore. He was asking a different question: What does Judaism say about this?

For about an hour, we talked about the Jewish meaning of a tattoo. We talked about how you shouldn't do anything with your body at *nineteen* that you might regret at *forty*. Having a tattoo is not like having a bad haircut or a bad suit. It stays with you.

We talked about how our sages thought that tattoos were a sign of slavery and paganism.

We talked about his grandmother, who is a Holocaust survivor. Knowing that Jews were forcibly tattooed in the concentration camps, how would she react to seeing her grandson with a tattoo? (That got to him.)

Finally, we discussed Judaism's belief that we don't own our bodies. We are merely "renting" them—from God. God owns our bodies, and we are not free to do anything with our bodies that we want to do, especially if we put ourselves in danger.

That includes tattoos, taking drugs, abusing alcohol, and smoking. Two weeks later, he came to see me again. He told me that our conversation had convinced him to cancel the tattoo appointment.

Jewish teenagers need to think about how Judaism views the body; and Jewish views of drugs, drinking, sexuality, abortion, and mercy killing; and the meaning of forgiveness in Judaism; and why we should still remember the Holocaust; and even the Jewish view of driver's education. All these are an essential part of what it means to be Jewish—and human—in our time.

If you drop out of religious school at the age of thirteen, you miss out on this entire conversation and on all this knowledge, wisdom, and tradition.

6. It shows that you can stay with a task. As a professor at a top women's college said, "Students should never learn that certain things can be done inadequately or incompletely [like Jewish education and activities]. That kind of belief is very damaging. They become *comfortable* with doing things in a halfhearted way. They have to learn the message: Whatever you do, *do well*."

7. Making bar or bat mitzvah the only thing in your Jewish life is similar to idolatry. You are probably thinking that idolatry is worshiping gods made of wood or stone. But here is another definition of idolatry: *Making anything in Judaism so big that it replaces God, overshadowing everything else and becoming of supreme importance.*

Or, to put it another way, it means losing a sense of balance. Concentrating *only* on bar or bat mitzvah at the expense of everything else in Judaism means that you are concentrating *only* on a small piece of our faith and tradition. Making that small piece of Judaism into something larger than the rest of it is idolatry.

Need I remind you that Abraham shattered his father's idols—at the age of thirteen?

You Need to Have Jewish Fun: Youth Groups, Camps, and Israel

It's not enough to continue just your Jewish education after bar and bat mitzvah. You need to have fun with other Jewish kids as well. Informal Jewish education and experiences are as important as formal Jewish education. Judaism is more than religious school. Jewish youth groups, Jewish camping, and Israel experiences are indispensable to being a well-balanced Jew.

So, join your local Jewish youth group. Go to a Jewish summer camp that is run by one of the major synagogue movements—the Union for Reform Judaism camps (such as Eisner and Crane Lake in Massachusetts; Harlam in the Pocono mountains of Pennsylvania; Goldman in Indiana; Coleman in Georgia; Greene Family Camp in Texas; Swig and Newman in northern California; and Kutz in upstate New York, to name a few), or Camp Ramah if you're Conservative (there are various Camp Ramahs all over the United States, for instance, in the Berkshire Mountains in New England; in the Pocono Mountains of Pennsylvania; in Georgia, Washington, and California; and there are also Camp Ramahs in Canada), or various Orthodox summer camps (such as Camp Yavneh in New Hampshire, or Camp Morasha in Pennsylvania).

(A sports camp that has a lot of Jewish kids is *not* a Jewish summer camp. A Jewish summer camp is a camp that emphasizes Jewish programming, learning, and worship along with sports, arts, and water activities.) Youth programs and Jewish summer camps are a great way to learn that Judaism is not only about ritual and intellect, but also about *community*.

Equally indispensable to a Jewish teenager is a trip to Israel. The Talmud says that the land of Israel is the place where heaven and earth touch. Going there is fun, joyful, and exciting. It is a place that moves us in ways that will stay with us forever.

But remember: a trip to Israel is not just another teen tour. Israel is not a Jewish Disney World or theme park. Learn everything you can learn about Israel before the trip—especially Israeli history, the geography of the Land, and some conversational Hebrew—and try to become part of a group that will help you relive and remember the experience when you return home. That is why I recommend Israel trips that are sponsored by Jewish youth movements. At their best, they are not simply *tours*. They are *pilgrimages*.

The Jewish community is increasingly recognizing the connection between bar and bat mitzvah and Israel, and not simply as a place for a ceremony. Jewish federations have become involved with such programs as "Gift of Israel," in which the local community subsidizes Israel trips. Families are encouraged to save money annually for trips to Israel to which local federations also contribute money. In place of traditional bar and bat mitzvah gifts, some families even ask their guests to contribute to an Israel trip fund for their child in honor of the bar or bat mitzvah.

You might be wondering: "Youth groups, camps, Israel trips: *Do they 'count' toward success in life?*" It's a sad question. Must *everything* in life promote an academic or career-related goal? What has happened to the sheer joy of living?

I don't like the question, but I do like the answer to it: Yes, Jewish experiences *do* "count." Colleges seek well-rounded students who have values and commitments. They're not just looking for strong academics or students with a long list of such extracurriculars as sports, debating, or playing a musical instrument. Being involved in synagogue youth groups or Jewish camping or Israel trips indicates that you care about higher values. It shows that you are aware of the larger society.

As a teenager in my synagogue recently said in a class I was teaching: "A Judaism that doesn't ask you to make any changes in your life is not Judaism."

So instead of just "coasting through" Judaism, imagine a Judaism that asks us to make changes in our lives. Moreover, *demand* a Judaism that requires such changes. Anything less is not Judaism.

Remember That Jewish Memory Has Power

Memory is the fundamental commandment of Jewish life. It defines who we are and links our past to our present and teaches us how to create the future.

Go on a memory quest. Learn your Hebrew name. Learn your parents' Hebrew names. If you were named for someone, research the qualities of that person. Remember the name of the city or village in "the old country" where your family came from. Learn the names of the great Jewish teachers of that city, and learn what they taught.

I will always remember something that happened to me at the Jewish Museum in New York many years ago. I saw an exhibit of Jewish ritual objects from Czechoslovakia. The Nazis had saved those items, intending them to be a permanent record of a dead people.

I found myself gazing at a Torah curtain that had once hung over the Holy Ark in the Altneuschul in Prague. The curtain was from 1608. Not only was this from the oldest synagogue in Europe, it was the oldest Torah curtain in Europe. I read the name of the person who had given the curtain to the Altneuschul more than three centuries ago—Natan Bar Yissachar, also known as Karpel Zaks. When I saw that name my eyes filled with tears and my hands began to shake. My mother's family was from Prague. Her maiden name was Karpel.

But don't think that if a distant relative of yours didn't give a Torah curtain to a historic synagogue in Prague, you then lack access to Jewish memory. Each of us is a descendant, and each of us is also an ancestor. Our task is not only to inherit memory but to also *create* memory.

- ✳ Do *you* know enough to create Jewish memories for your own children?

- ✳ Do *you* know enough to hold a seder when your grandparents and parents are gone?

- ★ Will *you* know how to teach your children the story of Chanukah? Will you know how to say *Kaddish*, the prayer for the dead?

- ★ Do *you* have a good sense of the flow and flavor of Jewish history?

A woman who was responsible for cleaning out the house of her recently deceased mother once told me, "The sterling silver and the minks meant nothing to me. When I saw the *haggadot* that we used at our seders, with the wine stains of long-forgotten seders on the pages, and with *matzah* crumbs still in the bindings, that's when I lost it."

Wrong.

That was when she *found* it.

. . . As Yogi Berra Said: "It Ain't Over Till It's Over"

On the Friday after a recent Thanksgiving, a young man who was a sophomore in college came to see me in my office. We had never met before. He had become bar mitzvah at my synagogue years before I had arrived. He told me this story:

> Bar mitzvah for me and my friends was a big party and expensive gifts and a lot of questions about "How much did you make?" I looked back on it and said to myself, "Where was the religious grandeur and the power?" I rebelled. At college, I've gotten involved with Native Americans. Their spirituality and religious ecstasy is what I've always wanted to find in Judaism.
>
> I went on the Sacred Run to support the rights of Native Americans. We ran across Canada and across Europe. Somehow we wound up at Auschwitz. My Native American friends said to me, "This is your tribe's place of overwhelming darkness. Will you lead us in a ceremony at this place?"
>
> I didn't know what to say. I called my mother collect—from Auschwitz!—and asked her to find the prayerbook that I got when I became bar mitzvah. It was somewhere in my room. Then I asked her to read me the transliteration of the *Kaddish* prayer, so that I could write it down and say it at Auschwitz.

"Rabbi," said the young man, "I want to come back to my people. I really want to find that spirit again. My Native American friends sent me back to my tribe."

The prophet Isaiah knew what he was doing when he named one of his children *Shear Yashuv*, which means "A Remnant Will Return." A remnant will. A remnant has. A remnant always will.

Be part of the remnant.

✶

Imagine your Jewish life for the next few years. What elements will be part of it? What would you want to do to be a better Jew?

_____

_____

Try this Jewish "life plan" exercise:
"In the area of Jewish learning, this is what I hope to accomplish . . ."

_____

_____

"In the area of *mitzvot,* these are some things that I want to be able to do . . ." _____

_____

_____

"In the area of worship, these are some goals . . ."

_____

_____

GLOSSARY

aliyah (plural, *aliyot*): literally, "going up." The ascent to the *bimah* to say the blessings over the Torah scroll.

amidah: literally, the "standing" prayer. The nineteen prayers that constitute the main body of Jewish liturgy; also known as *tefilah* and the *shemoneh esreh.*

Baruch shepetarani me-onsho shel zeh: The blessing traditionally said by the father at the occasion of his son becoming bar mitzvah: "Blessed is The One Who has now freed me from responsibility for this one."

bikur cholim: visiting the sick.

bimah: the raised platform in most synagogues where the service is conducted.

birchat ha-mazon: the Hebrew blessing that is said after the meal.

chesed: loving-kindness.

chumash (from *chameish*, "five"): the Pentateuch (Five Books of Moses), or a book containing the Pentateuch.

derashah: a brief exposition of the Torah portion for the week. Sometimes referred to as the *devar Torah*, "a word of Torah."

haftarah: literally, "completion." The reading of the section from the Prophets for a particular Shabbat.

halachah: literally, "the going." Traditional Jewish law.

havdalah: literally, "separation," "distinction." The ceremony that ends Shabbat.

kavvanah: sacred intention, the goal of Jewish prayer and worship.

ketuvim: the third section of the Jewish Bible (*Tanach*). Includes Psalms, Proverbs, Job, Song of Songs, Ruth, Lamentations, Ecclesiastes, and Esther.

Messianic Age: a future time in which the world will be perfect. Some believe that a Messiah—a special person brought by God—will bring that age. There will be world peace, all persecution will end, and everyone will believe in God. We Jews believe that every *mitzvah* we do helps bring in the Messianic Age.

midrash: literally, "the searching out." A rabbinic interpretation of a biblical verse.

mincha: the afternoon Jewish worship service.

Mishnah: the classic code of Jewish law, compiled in Israel about 200 C.E. by Rabbi Judah Ha-nasi (Judah the Prince).

mitzvah (plural, *mitzvot*): an obligation of Jewish life.

musaf: the "additional" prayer in traditional liturgy. Recalls the ancient sacrificial rites of the Temple (the *musaf* or additional sacrifices) and repeats some themes covered earlier in the prayer service.

neviim: the second section of the Jewish Bible. Consists of the prophetic and historical writings.

nichum aveilim: the *mitzvah* of comforting mourners.

parasha: the Torah portion of the week. Sometimes referred to as the *sedra*.

Pirke Avot: literally, "the chapters of the fathers." The ethical teachings of the Mishnah.

Shulchan Aruch: literally, "the set table." The sixteenth-century code of Jewish law compiled by the legal scholar and mystic Joseph Caro.

Talmud: literally, "learning." Commentaries and discussions of the Mishnah, compiled circa 450 C.E.–500 C.E. One Talmud was compiled in Palestine. This is called the Palestinian or Jerusalem Talmud, known as the *Yerushalmi*. The more authoritative Talmud was compiled in Babylonia, and is known as the Babylonian Talmud, or the *Bavli*.

Tanach: acronym for *Torah*, *Neviim* (the Prophets), and *Ketuvim* (the later Writings) that constitute the Jewish Bible.

tefilah: the general term for Jewish prayer.

Torah: literally, "teaching" or "direction." This can mean the first part of the Jewish Bible that is read from the scroll. In its broadest sense, it refers to all Jewish sacred literature and, by implication, to all of Judaism.

tzedakah: the *mitzvah* of giving to others.

A LIST OF PLACES FOR YOUR *TZEDAKAH*

The following is a list of organizations that do worthwhile *mitzvot*. It can be used in several ways. You may choose to give part of your bat or bar mitzvah gift money to a particular organization whose work is meaningful to you. You may choose to put certain organizations on a list that will accompany the bar or bat mitzvah invitations, suggesting that your guests donate to the groups of their choice in honor of your bar or bat mitzvah. Or, your family may volunteer to work for the organization and enrich the bar or bat mitzvah experience by making it an experiment in living *mitzvot*.

Soup kitchens for the homeless. Soup kitchens feed the poor and the homeless. Sometimes they feed entire families. Donate leftovers from your bar or bat mitzvah celebration. Consider how much smoked salmon and salad is thrown out on any Saturday afternoon after a bar or bat mitzvah party, and then consider how many hungry people walk around the streets of even the fanciest suburbs. It doesn't have to be that way. To find your local food bank, consult the "Social and Human Services" section of your Yellow Pages.

Some notable food banks:

* *Mary Brennan Interfaith Nutrition Network (INN),* 211 Fulton Avenue, Hempstead, NY 11550. (516) 486-8506. www.the-inn.org
* *Long Island Cares, Inc.,* 10 Davids Drive, Hauppauge, NY 11788. (631) 582-FOOD. Operates the Long Island Regional Food Bank, which distributes huge quantities of donated food to soup kitchens and hunger organizations throughout Long Island. www.licares.org

★ *Rachel's Table*, 633 Salisbury Street, Worcester, MA 01609. (508) 799-7600. Or c/o Jewish Federation of Greater New Haven, 360 Amity Road, Woodbridge, CT 06525. (203) 387-2424, ext. 325. Or 1160 Dickinson Street, Springfield, MA 01108. (413) 733-9165. This New England–based chain of food pantries picks up leftovers from *simchas* (celebrations) and distributes them to the needy. www.rachelstable.org

★ *Hebrew Union College*, The Brookdale Center, 1 West 4th Street, New York, NY 10012. (212) 674-5300. A one-night-a-week program to feed the homeless. www.huc.edu

Local Soviet Jewry committees. These groups often include the most caring and dynamic members of the Jewish community. Call your local Jewish federation or Jewish community center for information on locating your local Soviet Jewry committee. For details on the nearest chapter to you, contact the NCSJ: Advocates on Behalf of Jews in Russia, Ukraine, the Baltic States & Eurasia, 2020 K Street N.W., Suite 7800, Washington, DC 20006. (202) 898-2500. www.ncsj.org

Agencies that help the homebound Jewish elderly. Many aged live in terrible isolation in dreary apartments with many locks on their doors. There are more of them than most people think. Agencies organized to help these individuals include:

★ *Dorot*, 171 West 85th Street, New York, NY 10024. (212) 769-2850. *Dorot* means "generations"—generations of Jews together, bringing light into dark lives. Dorot operates a soup kitchen and distributes clothing to homebound elderly Jews. www.dorotusa.org

★ *Hatzilu Rescue Organization*, 45 Manetto Hill Road, Plainview, NY 11803. (516) 822-3288. Aids the Jewish poor and elderly of Long Island. www.hatzilurescue.org

★ *The Ark*, 6450 N. California Avenue, Chicago, IL 60645. (773) 973-1000. Offers extensive services to poor Jews, including dental and medical care, employment counseling, a food pantry, and help in getting social services. www.arkchicago.org

★ *Project Ezra,* 465 Grand Street, 4th Floor, New York, NY 10002. (212) 982-4124. Works with the Jewish elders on the Lower East Side of Manhattan. They also offer tours of that historic immigrant neighborhood. www.projectezra.org

Other organizations that do worthy things

✶ *ARMDI: American Friends of Magen David Adom*, 352 Seventh Avenue, Suite 400, New York, NY 10001. (212) 757-1627. The sole support arm in the United States for the Magen David, Israel's emergency medical and blood services organization. www.afmda.org

✶ *American Jewish Congress Legal Clinic*, Bernard Horwich Jewish Community Center, 3003 W. Touhy, Chicago, IL 60626. (847) 679-8289. Provides legal representation for those in need.

✶ *American Jewish World Service*, 45 W. 36th Street, 11th Floor, New York, NY 10018. (212) 792-2900. Has become the Jewish response to suffering caused by famine, epidemic, or natural disaster. The group has managed projects in Africa, South America, Mexico, and the United States. www.ajws.org

✶ *Bet Tzedek*, 145 S. Fairfax Avenue, Suite 200, Los Angeles, CA 90036. (323) 939-0506. Provides free legal work for poor Jews and non-Jews. Has produced a video, narrated by actress Bea Arthur, that portrays six examples of their work. www.bettzedek.org

✶ *The Blue Card*, 171 Madison Avenue, Suite 1405, New York, NY 10016. (212) 239-2251. Finds impoverished Holocaust survivors and provides them with direct financial support. www.bluecardfund.org

✶ *Chicago Chesed Fund*, 7045 N. Ridgeway, Lincolnwood, IL 60712. (847) 679-7799. Provides assistance for those in need of food, clothing, employment, and other living necessities. www.chicagochesedfund.org

✶ *The Eldridge Street Project*, 12 Eldridge Street, New York, NY 10002. (212) 219-0888. Established to preserve and restore the Eldridge Street Synagogue, one of the most beautiful older synagogues of New York City. Also plans to establish a Jewish historic cultural district on the Lower East Side. Deserves *tzedakah* because it preserves a valuable piece of our past. www.eldridgestreet.org

✶ *God's Love We Deliver*, 166 Avenue of the Americas, New York, NY 10013. (212) 294-8100. Prepares and delivers meals for people with AIDS. www.godslovewedeliver.org

✶ *Israel Bonds*. This and the UJC are the great international pillars of support for Israel. Israel's capital improvements and infrastructure are largely the result of the strong commitment to Israel Bonds by Jews all over the world. Not just *tzedakah*—it's an investment in Israel's future. Look in your local phone book for an office near you. The national headquarters is at 575 Lexington Avenue, 11th Floor, New York, NY 10022-6195. (212) 644-BOND. www.israelbonds.com

✦ *JACS*, 120 W. 57th Street, New York, NY 10019. (212) 397-4197. Provides resources for Jewish alcoholics, chemically dependent persons, and their significant others. Sponsors retreats and various spiritual support groups. There are many local branches of this organization. Check your phone book. www.jacsweb.org

✦ *Jewish AIDS Network of Chicago,* 3150 N. Sheridan Road, Apt. 10B, Chicago, IL 60657. (773) 275-2626. Provides services and referrals to those affected by HIV or AIDS. www.shalom6000.com/janc.htm

✦ *Jewish Big Brothers Big Sisters.* Volunteer program that provides a supportive environment for Jewish children. www.jbbbs.org

✦ *The Jewish Braille Institute of America*, 110 E. 30th Street, New York, NY 10016. (212) 889-2525. Provides books, tapes, special materials for summer camps, college and career counseling, and free *b'nai mitzvah* training to blind and partially sighted Jewish adults. Improves the quality of Jewish life for the estimated 20,000 Jewish blind and 50,000 Jews who are severely visually impaired. www.jewishbraille.org

✦ *Jewish Foundation for the Righteous*, 305 Seventh Avenue, 19th Floor, New York, NY 10001. (212) 727-9955. Many Christians who saved Jews from the Nazis now live in poverty in the United States, Europe, and Israel. Jews must remember them; our history is incomplete without them. The Foundation sustains them financially and emotionally, thus bearing witness to eternal gratitude. The Foundation has an excellent "twinning" program for bar and bat mitzvah (see chapter 5). www.jfr.org

✦ *Jewish National Fund*, 42 E. 69th Street, New York, NY 10021. (212) 879-9300. Improves and develops the land of Israel, most notably through the planting of trees. Virtually all forested land in the Jewish state is the gift of the JNF. This is one of the most important and most worthwhile ways of contributing to Israel. www.jnf.org

✦ *Lifeline for the Old—Yad LaKashish*, 14 Shivtei Israel Street, Jerusalem, 91000 Israel. 011-972-2-628-7829. Created so Jerusalem's elderly would create lovely handicrafts, *challah* covers, *talitot*, toys, metal *mezuzot*, ceramic items, clothing, book binding. Also employs young and old handicapped people. www.lifeline.org.il

✦ *MAZON*, 10495 Santa Monica Blvd., Suite 100, Los Angeles, CA 90025. (310) 442-0020. Asks Jews to send 3 percent of the cost of a *simcha* (celebration) to MAZON so we can share our blessing with the needy. MAZON, a Jewish response to hunger, then makes allocations to hunger organizations around the country. www.mazon.org

✦ *Myriam's Dream, Inc.* (203) 795-4580. Continues the inspirational work of the late Myriam Mendilow, who founded Lifeline for the Old in Jerusalem. Gives grants to elder centers and to elderly and disabled people who live in rural areas, small towns, and large cities. www.myriamsdream.org

✦ *National Institute for Jewish Hospice*, 732 University Street, North Woodmere, NY 11581. (800) 446-4448. The only national Jewish organization providing non-hospital alternatives for the terminally ill. Hospice is a place where people go to die with dignity and appropriate care. www.nijh.org

✦ *The National Yiddish Book Center*, Harry and Jeanette Weinberg Building, 1021 West Street, Amherst, MA 01002. (413) 256-4900. Yiddish must survive, and more than in small phrases. By finding, saving, and treasuring Yiddish books, the Book Center redeems a small part of the Jewish past. www.yiddishbookcenter.org

✦ *The New Israel Fund*, 1101 14th Street NW, 6th Floor, Washington, DC 20005. (202) 842-0900. Funds the following programs in Israel: Jewish/Arab relations; pluralism; civil rights and civil liberties; women's rights, especially rape crisis centers; and community action. www.nif.org

✦ *North American Conference on Ethiopian Jewry*, 132 Nassau Street, Suite 412, New York, NY 10038. (212) 233-5200. Helps Ethiopian Jews who have settled in Israel. www.nacoej.org

Shelters for battered Jewish women. Provide temporary shelter, counseling, and support services to Jewish women who are victims of domestic violence. Examples include:

✦ *Rebbetzin Chana Weinberg*, 398 Mt. Wilson Lane, Baltimore, MD 21208. (410) 486-0322. Operates one of fewer than ten Jewish battered women's shelters in North America. Contributions should be made out to Chana Weinberg Tzedakah Fund.

✦ *Shalva*, P.O. Box 46375, Chicago, IL 60646. (773) 583-HOPE (4673). Founded by Orthodox women who worked in a *mikveh* (ritual bath) and noticed scars on the women they were tending. www.shalvaonline.org

Other organizations

✱ *Simon Wiesenthal Center*, 1399 S. Roxbury Drive, Los Angeles, CA 90035. (310) 553-9036. Has taken a leading role in discovering Nazis in hiding as well as exposing modern hate groups. Insures that Americans will remember the Holocaust and its lessons. www.wiesenthal.com

✱ *Jewish Federations of North America*, Wall Street Station, P.O. Box 157, New York, NY 10268. (212) 284-6500. Most comprehensive Jewish charity in the world. Raises more than $2 billion annually from American Jews to serve the worldwide humanitarian needs of Jews. Jewish farmers in the Galilee, Jews in Eastern Europe, and those in Muslim nations all benefit from our giving. In individual communities, the combined UJA/Federation appeal gives funding to local communal needs—nursing homes, Jewish community centers, and various other social services. Giving to the UJC is absolutely essential for every serious Jew's *tzedakah* plans. www.ujc.org

With thanks to Rabbi Marc Gellman, Rabbi Bradley Shavit Artson, and Danny Siegel, who suggested many of the *tzedakot* on this list.

SUGGESTIONS FOR FURTHER READING

Adelman, Penina, Ali Feldman, and Shulamit Reinharz. *The JGirl's Guide: The Young Jewish Woman's Handbook for Coming of Age.* Woodstock, Vt.: Jewish Lights Publishing, 2005.

Feinstein, Edward. *Tough Questions Jews Ask: A Young Adult's Guide to Building a Jewish Life.* Woodstock, Vt.: Jewish Lights Publishing, 2003.

Kushner, Lawrence. *The Book of Miracles: A Young Person's Guide to Jewish Spiritual Awareness.* Woodstock, Vt.: Jewish Lights Publishing, 1997.

Mack, Stan. *The Story of the Jews: A 4,000-Year Adventure—A Graphic History Book.* Woodstock, Vt.: Jewish Lights Publishing, 2001.

Pearl, Judea, and Ruth Pearl, eds. *I Am Jewish: Personal Reflections Inspired by the Last Words of Daniel Pearl.* Woodstock, Vt.: Jewish Lights Publishing, 2005.

Salkin, Jeffrey K. *Putting God on the Guest List: How to Reclaim the Spiritual Meaning of Your Child's Bar or Bat Mitzvah.* 3rd ed. Woodstock, Vt.: Jewish Lights Publishing, 2005.

Sheinkin, Steve. *The Adventures of Rabbi Harvey: A Graphic Novel of Jewish Wisdom and Wit in the Wild West.* Woodstock, Vt.: Jewish Lights Publishing, 2006.

———. *Rabbi Harvey Rides Again: A Graphic Novel of Jewish Folktales Let Loose in the Wild West.* Woodstock, Vt.: Jewish Lights Publishing, 2008.

———. *Rabbi Harvey vs. the Wisdom Kid: A Graphic Novel of Dueling Jewish Folktales in the Wild West.* Woodstock, Vt.: Jewish Lights Publishing, 2010.

Shire, Michael. *The Jewish Prophet: Visionary Words from Moses and Miriam to Henrietta Szold and A. J. Heschel.* Woodstock, Vt.: Jewish Lights Publishing, 2002.

Spiegelman, Art. *The Complete Maus.* London: Penguin, 2003.

Taylor, Sydney. *All-of-a-Kind Family.* New York: Delacorte Books for Young Readers, 2005.

More for Teens

I Am Jewish
Personal Reflections Inspired by the Last Words of Daniel Pearl
Edited by Judea and Ruth Pearl

Almost 150 Jews—both famous and not—from all walks of life, from all around the world, write about identity, heritage, covenant/chosenness and faith, humanity and ethnicity, and *Tikkun Olam* and justice.

6 x 9, 304 pp, Deluxe PB w/ flaps, 978-1-58023-259-3 **$18.99**

Download a free copy of the *I Am Jewish Teacher's Guide* at our website:
www.jewishlights.com

The Book of Miracles: A Young Person's Guide to Jewish Spiritual Awareness   *By Lawrence Kushner*
Encourages kids' awareness of their own spirituality, revealing the essence of Judaism in a language they can understand and enjoy.
6 x 9, 96 pp, 2-color illus., HC, 978-1-879045-78-1 **$16.95**

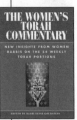

Spirituality/Women's Interest

The Divine Feminine in Biblical Wisdom Literature: Selections Annotated & Explained   *Translated & Annotated by Rabbi Rami Shapiro* 5½ x 8½, 240 pp, Quality PB, 978-1-59473-109-9 **$16.99** *(A book from SkyLight Paths, Jewish Lights' sister imprint)*

The Quotable Jewish Woman: Wisdom, Inspiration & Humor from the Mind & Heart   *Edited by Elaine Bernstein Partnow* 6 x 9, 496 pp, Quality PB, 978-1-58023-236-4 **$19.99**

The Women's Haftarah Commentary: New Insights from Women Rabbis on the 54 Weekly Haftarah Portions, the 5 Megillot & Special Shabbatot   *Edited by Rabbi Elyse Goldstein* 6 x 9, 560 pp, Quality PB, 978-1-58023-371-2 **$19.99**

The Women's Torah Commentary: New Insights from Women Rabbis on the 54 Weekly Torah Portions   *Edited by Rabbi Elyse Goldstein*
6 x 9, 496 pp, Quality PB, 978-1-58023-370-5 **$19.99**; HC, 978-1-58023-076-6 **$34.95**

The Year Mom Got Religion: One Woman's Midlife Journey into Judaism   *By Lee Meyerhoff Hendler* 6 x 9, 208 pp, Quality PB, 978-1-58023-070-4 **$15.95**

Spirituality/Crafts
(from SkyLight Paths, Jewish Lights' sister imprint)

Beading—The Creative Spirit: Finding Your Sacred Center through the Art of Beadwork   *By Wendy Ellsworth*
Invites you on a spiritual pilgrimage into the kaleidoscope world of glass and color.
7 x 9, 240 pp, 8-page full-color insert, b/w photos and diagrams, Quality PB, 978-1-59473-267-6 **$18.99**

Contemplative Crochet: A Hands-On Guide for Interlocking Faith and Craft   *By Cindy Crandall-Frazier; Foreword by Linda Skolnik*
Will take you on a path deeper into your crocheting and your spiritual awareness.
7 x 9, 208 pp, b/w photos, Quality PB, 978-1-59473-238-6 **$16.99**

The Knitting Way: A Guide to Spiritual Self-Discovery   *By Linda Skolnik and Janice MacDaniels* Shows how to use the practice of knitting to strengthen our spiritual selves. 7 x 9, 240 pp, b/w photos, Quality PB, 978-1-59473-079-5 **$16.99**

The Quilting Path: A Guide to Spiritual Self-Discovery through Fabric, Thread and Kabbalah   *By Louise Silk* Explores how to cultivate personal growth through quilt making. 7 x 9, 192 pp, b/w photos, Quality PB, 978-1-59473-206-5 **$16.99**

The Painting Path: Embodying Spiritual Discovery through Yoga, Brush and Color   *By Linda Novick; Foreword by Richard Segalman*
Explores the divine connection you can experience through art.
7 x 9, 208 pp, 8-page full-color insert, b/w photos, Quality PB, 978-1-59473-226-3 **$18.99**

The Scrapbooking Journey: A Hands-On Guide to Spiritual Discovery   *By Cory Richardson-Lauve; Foreword by Stacy Julian*
Reveals how this craft can become a practice used to deepen and shape your life.
7 x 9, 176 pp, 8-page full-color insert, b/w photos, Quality PB, 978-1-59473-216-4 **$18.99**

Holidays/Holy Days

Who by Fire, Who by Water—Un'taneh Tokef
Edited by Rabbi Lawrence A. Hoffman, PhD
Examines the prayer's theology, authorship and poetry through a set of lively essays, all written in accessible language.
6 x 9, 272 pp, HC, 978-1-58023-424-5 **$24.99**

Rosh Hashanah Readings: Inspiration, Information and Contemplation
Yom Kippur Readings: Inspiration, Information and Contemplation
Edited by Rabbi Dov Peretz Elkins; Section Introductions from Arthur Green's These Are the Words
An extraordinary collection of readings, prayers and insights that will enable you to enter into the spirit of the High Holy Days in a personal and powerful way, permitting the meaning of the Jewish New Year to enter the heart.
Rosh Hashanah: 6 x 9, 400 pp, Quality PB, 978-1-58023-437-5 **$19.99**; HC, 978-1-58023-239-5 **$24.99**
Yom Kippur: 6 x 9, 368 pp, Quality PB, 978-1-58023-438-2 **$19.99**; HC, 978-1-58023-271-5 **$24.99**

Jewish Holidays: A Brief Introduction for Christians
By Rabbi Kerry M. Olitzky and Rabbi Daniel Judson
5½ x 8½, 176 pp, Quality PB, 978-1-58023-302-6 **$16.99**

Reclaiming Judaism as a Spiritual Practice: Holy Days and Shabbat
By Rabbi Goldie Milgram 7 x 9, 272 pp, Quality PB, 978-1-58023-205-0 **$19.99**

7th Heaven: Celebrating Shabbat with Rebbe Nachman of Breslov
By Moshe Mykoff with the Breslov Research Institute
5⅛ x 8¼, 224 pp, Deluxe PB w/ flaps, 978-1-58023-175-6 **$18.95**

Shabbat, 2nd Edition: The Family Guide to Preparing for and Celebrating the Sabbath *By Dr. Ron Wolfson*
7 x 9, 320 pp, illus., Quality PB, 978-1-58023-164-0 **$19.99**

Hanukkah, 2nd Edition: The Family Guide to Spiritual Celebration
By Dr. Ron Wolfson 7 x 9, 240 pp, illus., Quality PB, 978-1-58023-122-0 **$18.95**

The Jewish Family Fun Book, 2nd Edition: Holiday Projects, Everyday Activities, and Travel Ideas with Jewish Themes *By Danielle Dardashti and Roni Sarig; Illus. by Avi Katz*
6 x 9, 304 pp, 70+ b/w illus. & diagrams, Quality PB, 978-1-58023-333-0 **$18.99**

The Jewish Lights Book of Fun Classroom Activities: Simple and Seasonal
Projects for Teachers and Students *By Danielle Dardashti and Roni Sarig*
6 x 9, 240 pp, Quality PB, 978-1-58023-206-7 **$19.99**

Passover

My People's Passover Haggadah
Traditional Texts, Modern Commentaries
Edited by Rabbi Lawrence A. Hoffman, PhD, and David Arnow, PhD
A diverse and exciting collection of commentaries on the traditional Passover Haggadah—in two volumes!
Vol. 1: 7 x 10, 304 pp, HC, 978-1-58023-354-5 **$24.99**
Vol. 2: 7 x 10, 320 pp, HC, 978-1-58023-346-0 **$24.99**

Leading the Passover Journey: The Seder's Meaning Revealed,
the Haggadah's Story Retold *By Rabbi Nathan Laufer*
Uncovers the hidden meaning of the Seder's rituals and customs.
6 x 9, 224 pp, Quality PB, 978-1-58023-399-6 **$18.99**; HC, 978-1-58023-211-1 **$24.99**

The Women's Passover Companion: Women's Reflections on the Festival of Freedom
Edited by Rabbi Sharon Cohen Anisfeld, Tara Mohr and Catherine Spector; Foreword by Paula E. Hyman
6 x 9, 352 pp, Quality PB, 978-1-58023-231-9 **$19.99**

The Women's Seder Sourcebook: Rituals & Readings for Use at the Passover Seder
Edited by Rabbi Sharon Cohen Anisfeld, Tara Mohr and Catherine Spector; Foreword by Paula E. Hyman
6 x 9, 384 pp, Quality PB, 978-1-58023-232-6 **$19.99**

Creating Lively Passover Seders: A Sourcebook of Engaging Tales, Texts & Activities
By David Arnow, PhD 7 x 9, 416 pp, Quality PB, 978-1-58023-184-8 **$24.99**

Passover, 2nd Edition: The Family Guide to Spiritual Celebration
By Dr. Ron Wolfson with Joel Lurie Grishaver 7 x 9, 416 pp, Quality PB, 978-1-58023-174-9 **$19.95**

Life Cycle
Marriage/Parenting/Family/Aging

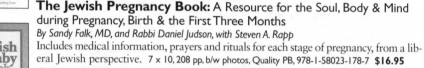

The New Jewish Baby Album: Creating and Celebrating the Beginning of a Spiritual Life—A Jewish Lights Companion
By the Editors at Jewish Lights; Foreword by Anita Diamant; Preface by Rabbi Sandy Eisenberg Sasso
A spiritual keepsake that will be treasured for generations. More than just a memory book, *shows you how—and why it's important*—to create a Jewish home and a Jewish life. 8 x 10, 64 pp, Deluxe Padded HC, Full-color illus., 978-1-58023-138-1 **$19.95**

The Jewish Pregnancy Book: A Resource for the Soul, Body & Mind during Pregnancy, Birth & the First Three Months
By Sandy Falk, MD, and Rabbi Daniel Judson, with Steven A. Rapp
Includes medical information, prayers and rituals for each stage of pregnancy, from a liberal Jewish perspective. 7 x 10, 208 pp, b/w photos, Quality PB, 978-1-58023-178-7 **$16.95**

Celebrating Your New Jewish Daughter: Creating Jewish Ways to Welcome Baby Girls into the Covenant—New and Traditional Ceremonies *By Debra Nussbaum Cohen; Foreword by Rabbi Sandy Eisenberg Sasso* 6 x 9, 272 pp, Quality PB, 978-1-58023-090-2 **$18.95**

The New Jewish Baby Book, 2nd Edition: Names, Ceremonies & Customs—A Guide for Today's Families *By Anita Diamant* 6 x 9, 336 pp, Quality PB, 978-1-58023-251-7 **$19.99**

Parenting as a Spiritual Journey: Deepening Ordinary and Extraordinary Events into Sacred Occasions *By Rabbi Nancy Fuchs-Kreimer*
6 x 9, 224 pp, Quality PB, 978-1-58023-016-2 **$16.95**

Parenting Jewish Teens: A Guide for the Perplexed
By Joanne Doades
Explores the questions and issues that shape the world in which today's Jewish teenagers live and offers constructive advice to parents.
6 x 9, 176 pp, Quality PB, 978-1-58023-305-7 **$16.99**

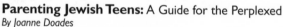

Judaism for Two: A Spiritual Guide for Strengthening and Celebrating Your Loving Relationship *By Rabbi Nancy Fuchs-Kreimer, PhD, and Rabbi Nancy H. Wiener, DMin; Foreword by Rabbi Elliot N. Dorff*
Addresses the ways Jewish teachings can enhance and strengthen committed relationships. 6 x 9, 224 pp, Quality PB, 978-1-58023-254-8 **$16.99**

The Creative Jewish Wedding Book, 2nd Edition: A Hands-On Guide to New & Old Traditions, Ceremonies & Celebrations *By Gabrielle Kaplan-Mayer*
9 x 9, 288 pp, b/w photos, Quality PB, 978-1-58023-398-9 **$19.99**

Divorce Is a Mitzvah: A Practical Guide to Finding Wholeness and Holiness When Your Marriage Dies *By Rabbi Perry Netter; Afterword by Rabbi Laura Geller*
6 x 9, 224 pp, Quality PB, 978-1-58023-172-5 **$16.95**

Embracing the Covenant: Converts to Judaism Talk About Why & How
By Rabbi Allan Berkowitz and Patti Moskovitz 6 x 9, 192 pp, Quality PB, 978-1-879045-50-7 **$16.95**

The Guide to Jewish Interfaith Family Life: An InterfaithFamily.com Handbook
Edited by Ronnie Friedland and Edmund Case
6 x 9, 384 pp, Quality PB, 978-1-58023-153-4 **$18.95**

A Heart of Wisdom: Making the Jewish Journey from Midlife through the Elder Years
Edited by Susan Berrin; Foreword by Harold Kushner
6 x 9, 384 pp, Quality PB, 978-1-58023-051-3 **$18.95**

Introducing My Faith and My Community: The Jewish Outreach Institute Guide for the Christian in a Jewish Interfaith Relationship
By Rabbi Kerry M. Olitzky 6 x 9, 176 pp, Quality PB, 978-1-58023-192-3 **$16.99**

Making a Successful Jewish Interfaith Marriage: The Jewish Outreach Institute Guide to Opportunities, Challenges and Resources *By Rabbi Kerry M. Olitzky with Joan Peterson Littman*
6 x 9, 176 pp, Quality PB, 978-1-58023-170-1 **$16.95**

So That Your Values Live On: Ethical Wills and How to Prepare Them
Edited by Jack Riemer and Nathaniel Stampfer
6 x 9, 272 pp, Quality PB, 978-1-879045-34-7 **$18.99**

About Jewish Lights

People of all faiths and backgrounds yearn for books that attract, engage, educate, and spiritually inspire.

Our principal goal is to stimulate thought and help all people learn about who the Jewish People are, where they come from, and what the future can be made to hold. While people of our diverse Jewish heritage are the primary audience, our books speak to people in the Christian world as well and will broaden their understanding of Judaism and the roots of their own faith.

We bring to you authors who are at the forefront of spiritual thought and experience. While each has something different to say, they all say it in a voice that you can hear.

Our books are designed to welcome you and then to engage, stimulate, and inspire. We judge our success not only by whether or not our books are beautiful and commercially successful, but by whether or not they make a difference in your life.

For your information and convenience, at the back of this book we have provided a list of other Jewish Lights books you might find interesting and useful. They cover all the categories of your life:

Bar/Bat Mitzvah
Bible Study / Midrash
Children's Books
Congregation Resources
Current Events / History
Ecology / Environment
Fiction: Mystery, Science Fiction
Grief / Healing
Holidays / Holy Days
Inspiration
Kabbalah / Mysticism / Enneagram

Life Cycle
Meditation
Men's Interest
Parenting
Prayer / Ritual / Sacred Practice
Social Justice
Spirituality
Theology / Philosophy
Travel
12-Step
Women's Interest

Stuart M. Matlins, Publisher

Or phone, fax, mail or e-mail to: **JEWISH LIGHTS Publishing**
Sunset Farm Offices, Route 4 • P.O. Box 237 • Woodstock, Vermont 05091
Tel: (802) 457-4000 • Fax: (802) 457-4004 • www.jewishlights.com
Credit card orders: (800) 962-4544 (8:30AM–5:30PM ET Monday–Friday)
Generous discounts on quantity orders. SATISFACTION GUARANTEED. Prices subject to change.

For more information about each book, visit our website at www.jewishlights.com